ONLY CHICKEN BREASTS

A COOKBOOK
by QUENTIN ERICKSON

ONLY CHICKEN BREASTS

Published by Entrée Press, LLC.

Copyright © 2011 Entrée Press, LLC. All rights reserved.

No part of the contents of this publication may be reproduced or transmitted by any means, electronic, mechanical, photocopying, recording, or otherwise without the written permission of Entrée Press, LLC.

ONLY CHICKEN BREASTS

ISBN 978-0-9773344-2-1

Printed in the United States of America

No liability is assumed with respect to the use of the information contained herein. Although all reasonable efforts have been made to present accurate information in the preparation of this publication, no guarantees, including expressed or implied warranties, are made with respect to this information by the publisher and author who also assume no legal responsibility for the accuracy of presentations, comments or other information, including any errors or omissions in this publication. The user is encouraged to seek out additional information on the proper handling of food and cooking safety from other sources if any questions or concerns arise. In addition, no liability is assumed and all liability is expressly declined for damages resulting from the use, misuse, or failure to use the information contained herein. Please use common sense, and always err on the side of safety.

Products and company names mentioned herein may be the trademarks of their respective owners.

For my wonderful wife, Mary, and my sons, Rene and Alex, who have joined me over the course of many years, enthusiastically, on this culinary journey.

And a sincere thank you to Doug Schenkelberg, my all-weather friend, who, for this project, provided consultation and sound advice on various aspects of cooking and recipes.

QUENTIN ERICKSON, is a globe-trotting, life-long foodie and improvisational cook who is bringing his mantra *"Variety in food is the spice of life!"* to all who love culinary adventure. His exploratory cookbooks focus on the myriad of options and wealth of inspiration available to us all.

Entrée Press Online

Visit www.EntreePress.com to explore additional "Play with your food!" interactive cookbooks.

CONTENTS

THE FIRST BITE

USING THE COOKBOOK — 8

PLAY WITH YOUR FOOD — 9
- SUBSTITUTION REVOLUTION — 9
- PLAYING DRESS-UP — 10
- TO GRILL OR NOT TO GRILL — 12
- TIME OUT — 13
- FINDING YOUR STYLE — 14

THE FLAVOR FRONTIER — 15
- YOU HAVE GOOD TASTE — 15
- 1-2-3 TRINITY — 16
- COOKING WITH HEAT — 16
- RUBS AND MARINADES AND BRINES, OH MY! — 17
- INSPIRATION IS WHERE YOU FIND IT — 19

WRESTLING RECIPES — 20
- LOOK BEFORE YOU LEAP — 20
- A PLACE FOR EVERYTHING — 21
- ANYONE CAN ADD, BUT CAN YOU SUBTRACT? — 21

TASTES LIKE (GREAT) CHICKEN — 21
- THE ORIGINAL WHITE MEAT — 21
- A TRIP TO THE MARKET — 22
- JUMPING OUT OF MY SKIN — 22
- BEATING THE BREAST — 22
- PROPER PREP — 23
- COOKING THE BREAST — 23
- SAFETY FIRST — 24

GRILLED CHICKEN BREASTS

BUTTER / LEMON CHICKEN BREASTS Marinate | Grill	29
CAJUN CHICKEN BREASTS Marinate | Grill	30
CITRUS / TERIYAKI CHICKEN BREASTS Marinate | Grill | Flattened	31
CUCUMBER / PEPPER RELISH CHICKEN BREASTS Marinate | Grill	32
CUMIN CHICKEN BREASTS Grill	33
GARLIC / HERB CHICKEN BREASTS Marinate | Grill	34
HONEY / MUSTARD CHICKEN BREASTS Marinate | Grill	35
HONEY / ORANGE CHICKEN BREASTS Marinate | Grill	36
HONEY | SOY SAUCE CHICKEN BREASTS Marinate | Grill	38
LEMON / BASIL CHICKEN BREASTS Marinate | Grill	39
LEMONADE CHICKEN BREASTS Marinate | Grill	40
ORANGE JUICE / MAPLE CHICKEN BREASTS Grill	41
ORANGE JUICE / RUM CHICKEN BREASTS Marinate | Grill	42
PINEAPPLE | BROWN SUGAR CHICKEN BREASTS Marinate | Grill	43
RASPBERRY CHICKEN BREASTS Marinate | Grill	44
RASPBERRY SAUCE CHICKEN BREASTS Grill | Flattened	45
SOUR CREAM CHICKEN BREASTS Marinate | Grill	46
SWEET / SOUR CHICKEN BREASTS Marinate | Grill	47
TOMATO SOUP / HONEY CHICKEN BREASTS Grill	48
VINEGAR / MAPLE SYRUP CHICKEN BREASTS Marinate | Grill	49

VINEGAR / DIJON CHICKEN BREASTS Marinate | Grill	50
VINEGAR / WHITE SUGAR CHICKEN BREASTS Marinate | Grill	51
VINEGAR | KETCHUP CHICKEN BREASTS Marinate | Grill	52

OVEN BAKED CHICKEN BREASTS

ARTICHOKE CHICKEN BREASTS Oven	58
BLUE CHEESE CHICKEN BREASTS Oven | Flattened	60
BLUE CHEESE / BACON CHICKEN BREASTS Oven	61
GREEN OLIVE CHICKEN BREASTS Oven	62
HONEY CHICKEN BREASTS Oven	63
HONEY / PINEAPPLE CHICKEN BREASTS Marinate | Oven	64
LEMON CHICKEN BREASTS Oven	65
LEMON CRISP CHICKEN BREASTS Oven	66
MUSHROOM CHICKEN BREASTS Oven	67
MUSHROOM / SOUR CREAM CHICKEN BREASTS Oven	68
ORANGE CHICKEN BREASTS Oven	69
PARMESAN CHICKEN BREASTS Oven	70
PEACH GLAZED CHICKEN BREASTS Oven	71
PINEAPPLE CHICKEN BREASTS Oven	72
SOUR CREAM CHICKEN BREASTS Oven	73
SOUR CREAM / SALSA CHICKEN BREASTS Oven	74
SPINACH STUFFED CHICKEN BREASTS Oven | Flattened	76

STOVE TOP CHICKEN BREASTS

CELERY / GARLIC CHICKEN BREASTS — 83
Stove Top

CHEDDAR CHEESE / WHITE WINE CHICKEN BREASTS — 84
Stove Top

CILANTRO / CREAM SAUCE CHICKEN BREASTS — 86
Stove Top

COCONUT / SPINACH CHICKEN BREASTS — 88
Stove Top

CORN / JALAPEÑO CHICKEN BREASTS — 89
Stove Top

CRANBERRIES / ORANGE CHICKEN BREASTS — 90
Stove Top

CRANBERRY / SOUR CREAM CHICKEN BREASTS — 91
Stove Top

CREAM / BRANDY CHICKEN BREASTS — 92
Stove Top

CREAM CHEESE CHICKEN BREASTS — 93
Stove Top

CUCUMBERS / MUSHROOMS CHICKEN BREASTS — 94
Stove Top

CURRY / COCONUT CHICKEN BREASTS — 96
Stove Top | Flattened

DILL / CREAM CHICKEN BREASTS — 97
Stove Top

LIME / BUTTER CHICKEN BREASTS — 98
Stove Top | Flattened

MUSHROOM / RED WINE CHICKEN BREASTS — 99
Stove Top | Flattened

MUSHROOM / SPINACH CHICKEN BREASTS — 100
Stove Top | Marinate

MUSHROOM / WHITE WINE CHICKEN BREASTS — 102
Stove Top

ONION SAUCE CHICKEN BREASTS — 104
Stove Top

ONION / SOUR CREAM CHICKEN BREASTS — 106
Stove Top

ORANGE / GARLIC CHICKEN BREASTS — 107
Stove Top

PISTACHIO / SCOTCH WHISKEY CHICKEN BREASTS — 108
Stove Top

SESAME SEED CHICKEN BREASTS Stove Top	Flattened	109
TARRAGON / CREAM CHICKEN BREASTS Stove Top	110
VEGETABLE CHICKEN BREASTS Stove Top	112

SLOW COOKER CHICKEN BREASTS

CREAM CHEESE / ITALIAN CHICKEN BREASTS Slow Cooker	117
CREOLE SAUCE CHICKEN BREASTS Slow Cooker	118
DRIED CHIPPED BEEF CHICKEN BREASTS Slow Cooker	119

APPENDIX 121

PLAYING WITH FIRE (INSIDE) 121
- OVEN COOKING 121
- STOVE TOP COOKING 122
- SLOW COOKER / CROCK-POT COOKING 123

PLAYING WITH FIRE (OUTSIDE) 124
- ABOUT COALS 124
- THREE GRILLING METHODS 125
- GRILL HEAT CONTROL 126
- GAS GRILLS 127
- GRILL SAFETY 127

AVOIDING THE EMERGENCY ROOM 127
- RUDE POISONING 127
- SAFE HANDLING OF PROTEINS 128
- AVOIDING CROSS-CONTAMINATION 128
- COOKING TEMPERATURES 129
- STOP, DROP AND ROLL 129

TABLES — 132
- TABLE 1: HERB AND SPICE SUBSTITUTIONS — 132
- TABLE 2: COMMON INGREDIENT SUBSTITUTIONS — 134
- TABLE 3: HEALTHY INGREDIENT SUBSTITUTIONS — 135
- TABLE 4: LIQUOR SUBSTITUTIONS — 136
- TABLE 5: SAFE INTERNAL TEMPERATURES — 136
- TABLE 6: TRINITY FLAVOR BASES — 137
- TABLE 7: PEPPERHEAD SCALE — 137
- TABLE 8: RECOMMENDED CHICKEN GEAR — 138
- REFERENCES — 139

INDEX — 141

THE FIRST BITE

"Cooking is like love. It should be entered into with abandon or not at all."
Harriet Van Horne

"I feel a recipe is only a theme, which an intelligent cook can play each time with a variation."
Madame Benoit

These two quotes eloquently encapsulate my personal philosophy on cooking and the intent of this cookbook. Cooking, like life, is a great adventure that should be undertaken with great gusto.

My hobby over the years has been collecting and cooking recipes, with a focus on the unusual, the outlandish and the novel. Early on, I found that I derived more satisfaction from experimentation than with following the "paint-by-numbers" method.

Substituting ingredients, altering ingredient amounts, changing cooking methods—it has all become a happy obsession. Some basic kitchen and grilling equipment, a well-stocked pantry and a vivid imagination can result in stellar cuisine.

As a result of this on-going experimentation, I have become a better cook, I have a lot more fun in the kitchen, and my palate has become much more refined. I believe that you too can achieve these same benefits by embracing an adventurous attitude. These recipes should be seen as the jumping-off point of *your* great adventure.

Explore, experiment, be bold and find inspiration in the subtle and the obvious. Cooking, as is life, is a journey whose path can be both sweet and savory and whose destination is satisfaction. When you pour your heart and soul into cooking, the rewards are immense.

USING THE COOKBOOK

As I experiment with my recipes, I do a pretty fair job of documenting substitutions and other alterations I've made, although sometimes the scribbles can be a bit indecipherable. The page formatting of the recipes in this collection is intended to directly assist you on your journey of exploration. Use these pages to shop for ingredients, capture the thoughts of dinner guests, document cooking dates, and most importantly, record your experimentation for future reference.

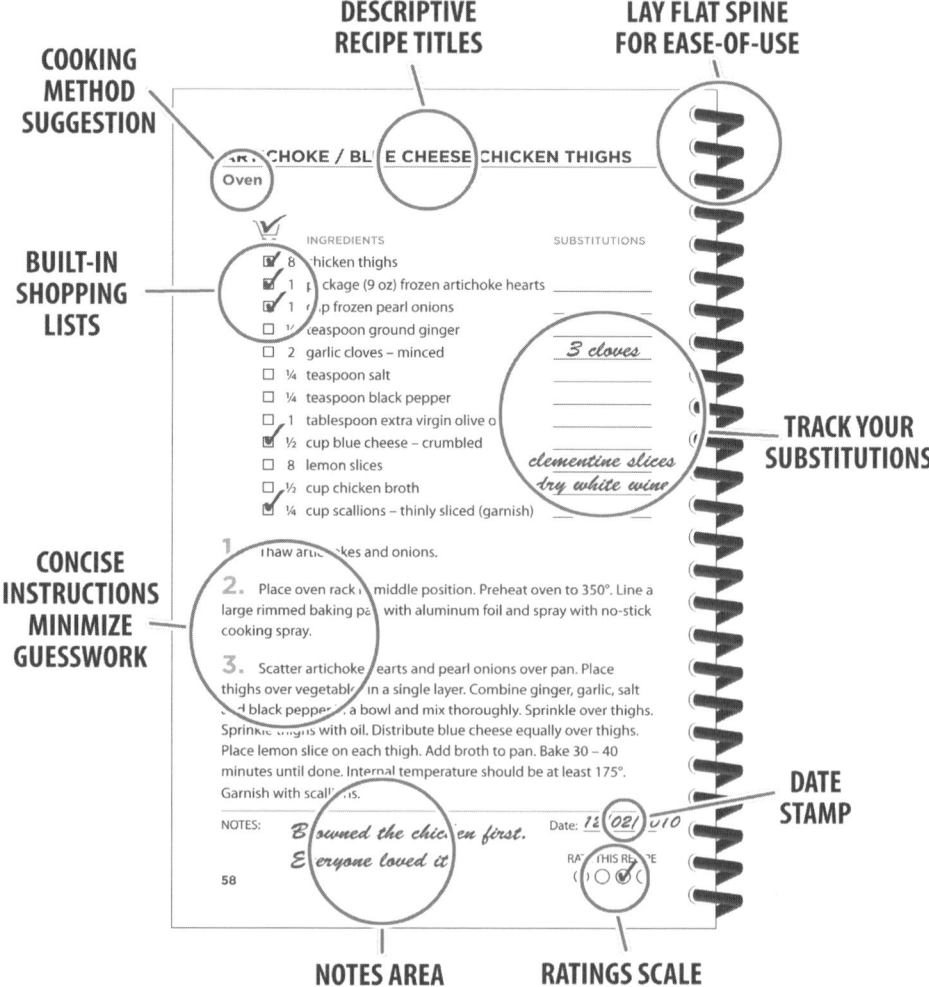

PLAY WITH YOUR FOOD

The ingredient, flavoring and cooking process combinations available to you are virtually infinite, bounded only by the ingredients you happen to have on hand. Take advantage of that variety. Recipes are but a framework to build upon and to deviate from, to alter and to modify to your own tastes and satisfaction.

Make adjustments and refinements to the recipe until the dish is perfect for you. It is a dash to the cupboard for spices, to the refrigerator for new ingredients or to the wine rack for a splash of wine. Experiment, enjoy, fail and then prevail. Innovate, experiment, compare recipes, combine recipes, feed the failures to the dog and the successes to royalty (your in-laws). Be bold. Do. Try. Win!

SUBSTITUTION REVOLUTION

Your primary method for creating culinary creations unique to you and your tastes is through ingredient substitution. Substitutions can have a subtle or profound impact on the flavor profile, texture, healthiness and even the cooking time of recipes. By fully embracing experimentation and improvisation, you will have more fun in the kitchen while becoming a better cook, you'll develop a more sophisticated palate, and you'll create a collection of recipes that are uniquely yours.

There are other reasons you might want to substitute an ingredient (other than for the sheer enjoyment of tasting your successful creations). You may have health concerns, you may be missing an ingredient, or you may not like a particular taste.

In the appendix, you'll find a wealth of information that will get you going in the right direction. The material is not exhaustive, nor is it meant to be. It represents only a small portion of the options available to you, but it will be a solid reference for you in your adventures. Use your imagination, improvise, explore!

Appendix – Table 1: Herb and Spice Substitutions

Appendix – Table 2: Common Ingredient Substitutions

Appendix – Table 3: Healthy Ingredient Substitutions

Appendix – Table 4: Liquor Substitutions

PLAYING DRESS-UP

Diners eat first with their eyes. If your food looks unappetizing, you've gotten off on the wrong taste bud. The way your meal is presented affects the way the diners think the food will taste.

The Plan

Preplan the presentation of the dish from the time you begin its preparation. Have a visualization of the completed meal in mind. If you are serving hot food, plating has to be done quickly. Consider building a "practice plate" before plating all the meals.

The Plate

Use a plate large enough to allow you to use "white space" as a design element. You don't want to crowd the food. Allow the food to "breathe" on the plate. Plates that are white or neural in color will allow the food to stand front and center. The shape of the plate should be simple as well. The focus should always be on the food.

Consider heating the plates in an electric oven if that particular food combination can benefit from a warm plate that keeps the components warm during serving and on into the meal. Preheat the oven to 150° and warm the plates for 5 minutes or so. Be extra careful handling the hot plates.

Pay attention to how the plate will be oriented when served. Use the front of the plate to highlight the main focus of the meal. If you are going to add height to the food, placing the height at the back of the plate will add to the appeal.

Plating

First and foremost, keep it simple. Unless you have a kitchen staff, you are going to want to be able to plate quickly, while the food is still hot. Start from the middle of the plate and work your way outward. Don't fuss too much with the plated food, you'll only make things worse.

COLOR: Select foods that add visual interest through color. Poultry and fish can have fairly bland colors. Colorful vegetables, peppers and fruit wedges can add that splash of color the plate is calling for.

SHAPE: Take the shape of the foods into consideration. Round meatballs, round Brussels sprouts and round potatoes on a plate do not an exciting plate make. Take a few moments to cut and shape the food into different figures and sizes to create visual appeal.

SYMMETRY: The house says odd always beats even: five meatballs are more pleasing to the eye than four; three colors on a plate are more interesting than two. Apply this maxim to any plating variable.

TEXTURE: Though not a visual presentation element, don't neglect texture. A well balanced plate requires variety in texture. Puréed squash, baked salmon and whipped potatoes may taste great together but will not provide any variety in mouth feel.

SAUCES: Go easy on the sauce, as too much sauce on the plate may give the impression that you are trying to hide a poorly prepared meal. Sauces are generally placed underneath the meat. If you lean the meat against the starch element of the meal, you'll keep the meat from becoming too saturated in the sauce, and the diner will better be able to view its preparation.

NEATNESS: And finally, take the time to be sure your plates are neat and free of drips and spills. No slopped sauces or stray pieces—your finished plate should be a work of art, with you the acclaimed artist.

Garnishes

Garnishes provide a great opportunity for adding that dash of panache. A quick shave of parmesan cheese, a sprig of parsley or cilantro, a wedge of avocado, a dollop of sour cream, a dash of paprika—all just a taste of the available garnishes. Garnishes are just the right touch of color, texture and flavor. All garnishes should be of the edible variety—avoid items like rosemary sprigs or flower pedals, for instance.

Inspiration

As always, inspiration is where you find it. Look to food magazines for ideas on arranging food on the plate, pay attention to the plating techniques at your favorite restaurant, and experiment with your own plates. You are only limited by attentiveness and imagination.

TO GRILL OR NOT TO GRILL

Chicken tartare is not an option. We know that chicken has to be cooked somehow. This cookbook provides suggested cooking methods for each recipe. These are only suggestions! Altering cooking methods is another opportunity for experimentation. These chicken recipes are generally interchangeable between oven, grill and slow cooker.

When cooking chicken in the oven, a relatively steady, even, medium temperature produces the best result. Chicken should not be cooked too quickly or too slowly. If cooked too quickly, it can become tough and dry. If cooked too slowly, the meat and skin can turn mushy.

If you plan on translating grill or oven recipes to the slow cooker, here are suggested recipe modifications:

- Reduce liquids by about 25 percent. There is very little evaporation in slow cooking.
- Reduce by approximately one half the recommended quantity of whole leaves and spices. Add additional herbs and spices in the last hour of cooking for a flavor boost.

Whatever cooking method you choose, the internal temperature of chicken should be at least 165°, and the juices should run clear. Use a meat thermometer to ensure doneness.

TIME OUT

Different situations can influence cooking times. For example, not all ovens are accurate—they can vary by many degrees plus or minus the set temperature. You will need to learn the idiosyncrasies of your particular oven.

Foods cook more slowly at higher altitudes, so depending on the nature of your oven and your altitude, cooking times could vary by as much as 20%.

If you use a convection oven, cooking times will definitely be different from those of a conventional oven. Refer to the manufacturers' recommendations about cooking times.

Cooking times for bone-in meats is longer as the bone absorbs a lot of heat and does not conduct heat effectively.

Meat that has been brined will cook more quickly. There is speculation that the extra moisture in the tissue, with its high heat conductivity qualities, accelerates the cooking process.

Other factors that influence cooking time include the thickness of the cut, temperature of the meat when you begin cooking, how many times you open the cooking equipment to take a peek, the quantity of other foods being cooked at the same time, and the fat content of the item being cooked.

A meat thermometer is now standard equipment in every kitchen. If you don't have one, pick one up the next time you leave the house! Using a meat thermometer is quite straight forward: place the probe in the thickest part of the cut and away from bone. See Table 5 in the Appendix for recommended safe internal temperatures for cooked meats.

FINDING YOUR STYLE

Perhaps the most enjoyable aspect of constant exploration and improvisation, other than the well-deserved accolades of dinner guests, is that through exploration you will be developing your own voice, your own brand of confidence, your own style.

"Style" in cooking has many faces. Do you prefer the comfort provided by comfort food and a satisfied brood? Do you concentrate on healthy fare and fresh produce? Does your idea of cooking involve stoking coals and managing the temperature of a grill, regardless of mother nature's plans?

Do you prefer quick and easy meals, your pantry overflowing with instant potatoes, instant rice and instant gratification? Do you prefer cooking everything from scratch, time at the market and in the kitchen be damned? Are you a study in culinary improvisation, working without a net, your pantry stocked with imported spices and exotic concoctions?

Do you define your style by an American regional cuisine? Cajun? New England? Southwestern? Or perhaps you prefer cooking with an international flair. French? Italian? Mexican? Szechuan?

Your individual cooking style will have elements of all of these definitions, and will continue to refine itself over time. As you develop your "style," be sure to place an emphasis on expanding your horizons. By bringing in influences from many sources, you'll develop a sense of the compatibility of different tastes, you will learn to intuitively develop your own recipes, and in the process, you will find more joy in the kitchen.

THE FLAVOR FRONTIER

YOU HAVE GOOD TASTE

You have good taste. That much is obvious—you're reading this cookbook! Developing your culinary palate will (and should) be a lifelong endeavor, and you should consider it one of the most gratifying journeys you will embark upon in life. I consider the ongoing development of my palate to be one of my life's great journeys.

Developing your palate is not as difficult as you might think. And it is not necessarily just about trying new foods. You can start by trying different varieties of foods you already enjoy. There are literally hundreds of varieties of cheeses, and multiple varieties of many basic vegetables. Go with what you know.

But eventually you will need to venture into the unknown. Give new and novel (to you) food the benefit of the doubt, and admit that someone, somewhere, must believe a particular item to be at least edible or it probably wouldn't be considered "food."

You may find delicious treats that you never knew existed, and you may find some food items that for you will be an acquired taste. Acquire that taste. A great pleasure of mine is turning palate-shy people into Brussels sprout eaters. Boiled until tender (the sprouts, not the people), sliced open and stuffed with blue cheese, crumbled bacon, and a grain or two of sea salt, then drizzled with olive oil and broiled until the cheese is bubbling—avowed sprouts haters will be lining up for the recipe!

Stop smoking, brush your tongue.

And finally, the more information you have, the better equipped you are to explore the culinary landscape. Seminars, foodie magazines, television shows, restaurants—inspiration is where you find it. Explore. Climb. Conquer!

1-2-3 TRINITY

A "trinity" is the combination of three essential ingredients as the flavoring base in a recipe, often created by sautéing a combination of any three aromatic vegetables, condiments, seasonings, herbs, or spices. Trinities are most typically used when creating sauces, soups, stew, and stir-fries.

Geographic regions often have a trinity of ingredients that comprise the flavor base of dishes for that cuisine. For example, if the recipe calls for a base of onion, bell pepper and celery it is a good bet it is a Louisiana Creole dish. This particular trinity combination is known as the "Holy Trinity." Create your own regional dishes by experimenting with "trinity" combinations of ingredients. See Table 6 in the Appendix for a list of trinity flavor bases from various cultures.

COOKING WITH HEAT

To regulate the heat in a recipe, increase or decrease any of the heat ingredients listed here. With the exception of horseradish and wasabi, they are chili pepper-based.

- Hot pepper sauce is a primary heat source in many recipes. It is basically chili peppers combined with tomatoes, onions, vinegar, sugar and spices.
- Cayenne pepper is a powder derived from several different chilies to produce a hot, fiery taste.
- Red pepper flakes are available as whole flakes, ground red pepper flakes or crushed red pepper flakes.
- Harissa sauce is a product from north Africa. It is flavorful and hot. It is made up of hot chili peppers, cumin, coriander, garlic, caraway and oil.
- Sriracha is the name of a hot sauce with a southeast Asian influence. It is a hot chili sauce made from dried chilies ground into a paste with garlic, vinegar, salt, sugar and other ingredients.

- Horseradish, commercially prepared, is recommended in this cookbook because it is handy and convenient. For a real jolt, though, try freshly-grated horseradish root.
- Wasabi, horseradish's Japanese cousin, will give a good jolt, too.

The heat of peppers can be softened by removing the seeds and ribs from the inside, but the flesh will still be hot. In general, the smaller the pepper and the narrower the shoulder near the stem, the hotter the bite, but some varieties will break the rules with a fiery surprise.

When working with fiery peppers, it's important to protect yourself by using eye protection and wearing latex or rubber gloves. After handling peppers, wash your hands carefully with plenty of soap and warm water before touching your eyes and mouth.

In the event the heat surpasses your tolerance level, a cold glass of milk—not water—can have a mitigating effect on the condition. Milk contains the protein casein which pulls the capsaicin (the active heat component of chili peppers) away from the burning taste buds. See Table 7 in the Appendix for a list of capsaicin levels in different peppers.

RUBS AND MARINADES AND BRINES, OH MY!

Rubs

Spice rubs can add a great deal of flavor to meat or fish dishes. The spices are generally course ground, and the mixture can also include various herbs, salt and crushed garlic. Adding sugar will cause the rub to caramelize during cooking. Adding oil will create a paste, which can help the rub adhere to the meat. Rubs are readily available at the supermarket, but creating your own is much more rewarding. Rubs can be sweet, spicy and everything in between. If you are adventurous, rubs on vegetables can be delicious.

Generally, the rub should not be applied any sooner than two hours before cooking, although some recipes recommend longer times. The rationale for applying the rub just before cooking is to eliminate the chance of the rub inducing texture changes in the meat.

I've found that brushing the food item with spicy mustard just prior to applying the rub not only helps the rub stick but also adds complexity of flavor.

Place the food item on a cooking rack and lay newspaper under the rack. The rub should be applied generously. What sticks on, sticks on, and what falls off, falls off. I have found that using a pizza red pepper flake shaker works great for dispensing the rub. Gently massaging the rub onto the surface will increase the amount of rub that adheres. Apply the rub to the top, bottom and edges of the food item. Minimize handling—the more you fuss, the more the rub will fall off. Reapply the spices that dropped onto the newspaper to minimize waste.

Marinades

Marinating is the process of flavoring food by soaking in heavily seasoned liquid before cooking. A marinade can be acidic if based on liquids such as vinegar or lemon juice, or enzymatic if made with ingredients such as papaya or pineapple.

The maximum marinating time for poultry, under any circumstances, is 3 hours. Any longer than 3 hours and the meat will become mushy. I recommend 8 hours marinating for ribs. Marinade can be used to tenderize tough cuts of meats, but marinate times are quite long when trying to tenderize (up to 24 hours), so is recommended for only the toughest cuts.

Flavors can be enhanced with sweeteners such as sugar, honey and syrups. Soy sauce is a fantastic marinade ingredient. Herbs and spices commonly used in marinating are oil-soluble and their flavor is released when mixed with oil.

When marinating, use a jumbo re-sealable plastic bag to hold the marinade and meat. Before placing the bag in the refrigerator, set the bag on a plate to avoid a mess in the event of a bag leak. If the meat cuts are too large for the bag, cut the meat to fit. If jumbo bags are not available, any container will work if it can be sealed tightly.

Brines

Like marinating, brining is a process in which poultry, pork or seafood is soaked in a liquid solution before cooking. Meats with high fat content like beef, lamb and duck, tend not to benefit from brining. The basic brine is salt, sugar and water. I prefer sea salt and brown sugar, as they impart more flavor. Combine the ingredients in a ratio of 1 cup salt, 1 cup sugar to 2 quarts water.

Determine how much brine you'll need to completely submerge the food item in your selected, sealable container. Mix the salt, sugar and water (plus any other spices) together, heat the mixture to dissolve the salt and sugar, and let cool completely. Combine the brine and food in the container, and then place a ceramic plate or bowl on the food to submerge it, and place in the fridge. For large items like a whole turkey, use a cooler, adding ice to the cooler to keep it chilled for 8 to 12 hours. For small birds or poultry portions, brine for around 3 hours, and for pork chops or tenderloins, brine for around 6 hours.

The salt in the brine works to hydrate the cells of the muscle tissue by drawing water into the tissues through osmosis, and also denatures the cell proteins, further helping the meat to retain moisture during cooking.

Regardless of the science involved, it works! If you've never brined a turkey, you've missed a moist, mystical experience. Because a brine opens up the meat to hydration, if you add other herbs and spices to the brine, these additional flavor additives with also deeply infuse into the meat.

INSPIRATION IS WHERE YOU FIND IT

I traveled the globe during my hitch in the Navy, and I traveled the width and breadth of the United States in my decades-long civilian career. I have been privileged to experience a bounty of diverse foods and cultures, and to share those experiences with many friends, customers and employees.

Some "not-to-be-forgotten" culinary experiences include:

- A black bean soup in Indianapolis, Indiana
- Crawfish in restaurants along Lake Pontchartrain, Louisiana
- Baby back ribs in San Antonio, Texas
- A turtle soup in St. Louis, Missouri
- A steak flambé in a second-story restaurant overlooking the Ramblas in Barcelona, Spain
- Oysters in a bar in Athens, Greece
- Abalone on the wharf in San Francisco, California
- A crème brûlée at the Ritz-Carlton in Chicago, Illinois
- A gumbo in Greenfield, North Carolina
- A hearts of palm salad at the Breakers Hotel in West Palm Beach, Florida
- A rack of lamb in Neenah, Wisconsin

  ... and the list goes on

I ate fine and not-so-fine food as I dined at a myriad of restaurants and resorts. These experiences all had an impact on my personal cooking style. Always, I would try to choose a menu item that would give me a new experience. These unique dishes provided ideas and inspiration. Inspiration is where you find it. Use the skills of others to your own advantage.

WRESTLING RECIPES

LOOK BEFORE YOU LEAP

A highly recommended practice is to scan and survey a recipe before cooking it. You don't want to find midway though cooking that you are missing a key ingredient or that you are about to add an ingredient you don't like! Gather your ingredients and plan your substitutions.

A PLACE FOR EVERYTHING

The French term "mise en place" literally means "putting in place." For us it means organizing and arranging all ingredients for a recipe, prior to cooking, and placing them in the food preparation area in the order listed in the recipe. I also pre-measure all the ingredients and place them in small bowls or cups to use in sequence as I prepare a recipe.

ANYONE CAN ADD, BUT CAN YOU SUBTRACT?

It is simple to revise the profile of a recipe by adding or adjusting ingredients. Once all the ingredients are mixed, however, it is very difficult to eliminate or mask a flavor. Exercise a bit of caution when substituting ingredients — add a bit at a time and taste as you go.

TASTES LIKE (GREAT) CHICKEN

THE ORIGINAL WHITE MEAT

Growing up in the 1940s and 1950s, I, sadly, remember chicken breasts as diminutive, dry and tasteless. Today's chicken breast are gigantic, succulent and flavorful—a distinct turnabout. Breasts are the second most popular cut of the chicken, losing the first spot to the wildly popular wing. And, with the skin off, they are low in saturated fat, carbohydrates and calories and thus a favorite of diabetics and the health conscious.

From a versatility standpoint, chicken breasts are a personal favorite cut of meat. They can be grilled, broiled, baked, roasted and pan fried. They can be flattened, breaded, rolled and stuffed. They can be cooked skin on or skin off, and if you leave the skin on, butter, herbs and spices can be loaded underneath the skin. And they take to rubs, marinades and sauces like they were made for them.

A TRIP TO THE MARKET

When buying raw, prepackaged chicken breasts, make sure the cellophane is not ripped and that the package is not leaking. Do not purchase if there is liquid in the bottom of package. Avoid chicken breasts with any odor, or that appear to be bruised, off color or torn.

Cutlets are boneless chicken breasts that have been pounded to produce a tender piece of meat with a uniform thickness. They are usually boneless and skinless. Fillets are boneless strips that have been sliced from the breast. Tenderloin is the upper portion of the breast that runs along both sides of the breastbone.

JUMPING OUT OF MY SKIN

Skin on or skin off? Cooking chicken breasts with the skin on has some positives. The skin provides flavor, can hold marinades and rubs, and allows you to load herbs and spices between the meat and skin. The skin helps to keep the breasts moist. I always leave the skin on for grilling and recommend you do the same—the skin protects the meat from burning.

Removing the skin results in a reduction in calories, saturated fat and cholesterol. Diabetics and others with health concerns about weight control are advised to remove skin and excess fat.

Another option is to cook the breasts with the skin on and remove before eating.

BEATING THE BREAST

There are situations where it is desirable to take that fat chicken breast down a few notches. There are two types of flattened breast recipes in this collection—flattened for filling and flattened to facilitate the cooking process.

Breasts that will have a filling should be flattened, gently, to ⅓ to ½ inch thickness. For other flattened recipes, pound breasts gently until they are about 1 – 1½ inch in thickness.

Monitor the cooking of flattened breasts carefully. They cook faster than breasts that have not been flattened.

To control the meat as breasts are pounded, place breasts inside a re-sealable plastic bag or between two layers of plastic wrap. The flat end of a meat mallet may be used to gently, directly flatten the breasts.

A second—and in my opinion superior—technique is to place a 10-inch square, ½ inch thick wooden board or a piece of heavy-duty cardboard over the re-sealable bag and meat, and then use the mallet to flatten the meat to the desired thickness. The board or cardboard will equally distribute the impacts over the breasts, producing an even thickness and reducing the possibility of shattering the meat.

PROPER PREP

- Breast halves, or split breasts, are portions that have been split lengthwise to produce two "breast" cuts from a single chicken. Six medium size breasts will weight about 2 pounds; each breast weighs 5 – 6 ounces. All recipes in this collection are designed to serve four people. That is 4 – 6 medium size chicken breast halves, or approximately 2 pounds.
- Wash hands before and after handling the chicken breasts.
- Rinse breasts to remove extraneous material and pat dry with paper towels. Thoroughly dry the breasts to achieve proper browning. Rinsing does not kill bacteria—cooking to 165° kills bacteria.

COOKING THE BREAST

- Monitor cooking of breasts until the meat is no longer pink, juices run clear and internal temperature is at least 165°. Use a meat thermometer to obtain precise temperatures. The cooking times recommended in these recipes are approximations.

- Different sizes and shapes of breasts will require different cooking times. Flattened breasts will cook quicker than other breasts. For best results, uniform size breasts should be cooked together as different sizes require different cooking times.

- When breasts are fully cooked, remove from heat and rest the breasts by placing them on a clean plate and tenting with aluminum foil. Letting the breasts rest 5 – 10 minutes will allow juices to meld with the meat.

SAFETY FIRST

- Internal temperature of breasts should be at least 165° with no observable pink.

- Monitor cooking carefully. Cooking times can vary widely depending on the size and thickness of breast. Use a meat thermometer for an accurate measurement. The cooking times recommended in recipes are approximations.

- Once cooked, breasts should be kept either hot or promptly refrigerated or frozen.

- Cooked breasts can be cooled, covered and refrigerated for up to two days.

- Frozen uncooked breasts should be used within two or three months of freezing. Frozen cooked breasts should be used within one month.

- Reheat breasts in a covered baking dish in a 375° oven or in a microwave set on high until meat internal temperature is 165°.

NOTES

GRILLED
CHICKEN BREASTS

BUTTER / LEMON CHICKEN BREASTS
Marinate | Grill

	INGREDIENTS	SUBSTITUTIONS
☐ 4 – 6	skin-on chicken breasts	
☐ ½	stick butter	_____
☐ ½	cup lemon juice	_____
☐ 1	teaspoon dried minced onion	_____
☐ 1	teaspoon dry dill weed	_____
☐ ¼	teaspoon salt	_____
☐ ¼	teaspoon black pepper	_____

1. Melt butter in a saucepan. Combine all ingredients except breasts in a bowl and blend thoroughly. Reserve and refrigerate one quarter cup mixture for basting while grilling. Add remaining mixture to a re-sealable plastic bag. Pierce each breast 6 – 8 times with a fork. Add breasts to bag. Seal and toss to coat thoroughly. Marinate 3 hours in refrigerator. Turn bag occasionally to coat breasts evenly.

2. Lightly oil grill grates with no-stick cooking spray. Prepare grill for medium-direct heat. Place breasts on grill. Brush frequently with reserved marinade. Grill breasts on each side until done. Internal temperature should be at least 165°.

3. Platter breasts, wrap with foil and seal tightly until ready to serve.

NOTES: Date: _____

RATE THIS RECIPE
○ ○ ○ ○ ○

CAJUN CHICKEN BREASTS
Marinate | Grill

	INGREDIENTS	SUBSTITUTIONS
☐ 4 – 6	skin-on chicken breasts	
☐ 2	tablespoons Cajun seasoning	_____
☐ 2	tablespoons extra virgin olive oil	_____
☐ ¼	teaspoon black pepper	_____
☐ ¼	teaspoon salt	_____
☐ ½	teaspoon ground ginger	_____
☐ 2	garlic cloves – minced	_____
☐ ½	teaspoon onion powder	_____

1. Combine all ingredients except breasts to create rub. Pierce each breast 6 – 8 times with a fork. Massage breasts thoroughly with rub. Place breasts in a re-sealable plastic bag. Seal bag and refrigerate 3 hours. Turn bag occasionally to coat breasts evenly.

2. Lightly oil grill grates with no-stick cooking spray. Prepare grill for medium-direct heat. Place breasts on grill. Grill breasts on each side until done. Internal temperature should be at least 165°.

3. Platter breasts, wrap with foil and seal tightly until ready to serve.

NOTES: Date: _____

RATE THIS RECIPE
○ ○ ○ ○ ○

CITRUS / TERIYAKI CHICKEN BREASTS
Marinate | Grill | Flattened

	INGREDIENTS	SUBSTITUTIONS
☐ 4 – 6	skin-on chicken breasts	
☐ 2	tablespoons lemon zest	_____
☐ 2	tablespoons lemon juice	_____
☐ 2	tablespoons orange zest	_____
☐ 2	tablespoons orange juice	_____
☐ ½	bottle (10 ounce) teriyaki marinade	_____
☐ ½	teaspoon ground ginger	_____
☐ ¼	teaspoon salt	_____
☐ ¼	teaspoon black pepper	_____

1. Place each breast between sheets of plastic wrap and gently pound flat to an even 1 – 1½ inch thickness.

2. Combine all ingredients except breasts in a re-sealable plastic bag. Mix thoroughly. Add breasts to bag. Seal and refrigerate 3 hours. Turn several times during marinating process to coat breasts evenly.

3. Remove breasts from bag. Set aside. Pour marinade into saucepan. Bring marinade to boil, reduce heat and simmer 5 minutes.

4. Spray grill grate with no-stick cooking spray. Prepare grill for low-indirect heat. Place breasts on grill. Turn and baste with marinade several times while grilling. Grill covered until breasts are done. Internal temperature should be at least 165°.

5. Platter breasts, wrap with foil and seal tightly until ready to serve.

NOTES: 	Date: _____

RATE THIS RECIPE
○ ○ ○ ○ ○

CUCUMBER / PEPPER RELISH CHICKEN BREASTS
Marinate | Grill

	INGREDIENTS	SUBSTITUTIONS
☐ 4 – 6	skin-on chicken breasts	
☐ ½	small yellow bell pepper – chopped	_____
☐ 1	cucumber – peeled/seeded/chopped	_____
☐ 1	small onion – chopped	_____
☐ 1	tablespoon chopped fresh parsley	_____
☐ ¼	teaspoon red pepper flakes – crushed	_____
☐ 1	teaspoon chili powder	_____
☐ ½	teaspoon ground cumin	_____
☐ 2	tablespoons extra virgin olive oil	_____

1. Prepare relish by mixing together bell pepper, cucumber, onion, parsley and red pepper flakes in a medium bowl. Taste, adjust flavoring. Refrigerate.

2. Mix chili powder and cumin with oil in a small bowl. Pierce each breast 6 – 8 times with a fork. Massage mixture evenly over breasts and place in a re-sealable plastic bag. Marinate in refrigerator 3 hours. Turn bag occasionally to coat breasts evenly.

3. Lightly oil grill grates with no-stick cooking spray. Prepare grill for medium-direct heat. Place breasts on grill. Grill breasts on each side until done. Internal temperature should be at least 165°.

4. Serve with cucumber relish from Step 1.

NOTES: Date: _____

RATE THIS RECIPE
○ ○ ○ ○ ○

CUMIN CHICKEN BREASTS
Grill

	INGREDIENTS	SUBSTITUTIONS
☐ 4 – 6	skin-on chicken breasts	
☐ 1	teaspoon ground cumin	_____
☐ ½	teaspoon garlic salt	_____
☐ ¼	teaspoon salt	_____
☐ ¼	teaspoon black pepper	_____
☐ 2	tablespoons extra virgin olive oil	_____

1. Combine cumin, garlic salt, salt and black pepper in a re-sealable plastic bag and mix thoroughly. Brush breasts with oil. Add breasts to plastic bag and toss to coat thoroughly with seasoning mixture.

2. Prepare grill for medium-direct heat. Spray grill grate with no-stick cooking spray. Grill breasts on each side until done. Internal temperature should be at least 165°.

3. Platter, wrap with foil, seal tightly and rest 5 minutes.

NOTES: Date: _____

RATE THIS RECIPE
○ ○ ○ ○ ○

GARLIC / HERB CHICKEN BREASTS
Marinate | Grill

		INGREDIENTS	SUBSTITUTIONS
☐	4 – 6	skin-on chicken breasts	
☐	4	garlic cloves – minced	_____
☐	½	teaspoon dried oregano	_____
☐	1	teaspoon dried thyme	_____
☐	1	teaspoon dried basil	_____
☐	¼	teaspoon dried parsley	_____
☐	1	cup extra virgin olive oil	_____
☐	¼	cup white sugar	_____
☐	½	tablespoon honey	_____
☐	½	teaspoon cayenne pepper	_____
☐	¼	teaspoon salt	_____

1. Place all ingredients except breasts in a re-sealable plastic bag. Blend thoroughly. Pierce each breast 6 – 8 times with a fork. Add breasts to bag and coat thoroughly. Seal bag and marinate breasts in refrigerator 3 hours. Turn bag occasionally to coat breasts evenly.

2. Lightly oil grill grates with no-stick cooking spray. Preheat grill for medium-direct heat. Place breasts on grill. Grill breasts on each side until done. Internal temperature should be at least 165°.

3. Platter breasts, wrap with foil and seal tightly until ready to serve.

NOTES: Date: _____

RATE THIS RECIPE
○ ○ ○ ○ ○

HONEY / MUSTARD CHICKEN BREASTS

Marinate | Grill

		INGREDIENTS	SUBSTITUTIONS
☐	4 – 6	skin-on chicken breasts	
☐	½	cup extra virgin olive oil	_____
☐	½	cup orange juice	_____
☐	1	garlic clove – minced	_____
☐	1	can (8 ounce) tomato sauce	_____
☐	¼	cup cider vinegar	_____
☐	1	teaspoon dried leaf oregano – crushed	_____
☐	¼	teaspoon black pepper	_____
☐	1	teaspoon dry mustard	_____
☐	¼	cup honey	_____

1. Combine all ingredients except breasts, mustard and honey in a re-sealable plastic bag. Mix thoroughly. Taste, adjust flavoring. Reserve and refrigerate one third cup for basting later. Pierce each breast 6 – 8 times with a fork. Add breasts to bag and seal. Refrigerate and marinate 3 hours. Turn bag occasionally to coat breasts evenly.

2. Lightly oil grill grates with no-stick cooking spray. Prepare grill for medium-direct heat. Place breasts on grill. Brush with one third cup reserved marinade and turn frequently. Grill breasts on each side until done. Internal temperature should be at least 165°.

3. Combine honey and mustard in a bowl and brush on breasts just before serving.

NOTES: Date: _____

RATE THIS RECIPE
○ ○ ○ ○ ○

HONEY / ORANGE CHICKEN BREASTS
Marinate | Grill

		INGREDIENTS	SUBSTITUTIONS
☐	4 – 6	skin-on chicken breasts	
☐	½	cup honey	_____
☐	½	cup orange juice	_____
☐	½	cup chicken broth	_____
☐	½	tablespoon cider vinegar	_____
☐	½	tablespoon lemon juice	_____
☐	½	teaspoon grated orange zest	_____
☐	½	tablespoon soy sauce	_____
☐	1	teaspoon ground ginger	_____
☐	¼	teaspoon black pepper	_____
☐	1	tablespoon cornstarch	_____
☐	2	tablespoons water	_____

1. Combine all ingredients except breasts, cornstarch and water in a saucepan and bring to a boil. Remove from heat and cool. Taste, adjust flavoring.

2. Pour three quarter cup marinade into a re-sealable plastic bag. Place remaining marinade in a bowl and set aside in refrigerator. Pierce each breast 6 – 8 times with a fork. Add breasts to bag. Seal bag and toss to coat thoroughly. Marinate 3 hours in refrigerator. Turn bag occasionally to coat breasts evenly.

3. Lightly oil grill grates with no-stick cooking spray. Prepare grill for medium-direct heat. Place breasts on grill. Grill breasts on each side until done. Internal temperature should be at least 165°.

4. Combine water and cornstarch in a small saucepan and cook until smooth. Add refrigerated marinade. Bring to a boil, reduce heat and simmer until thickened. Pour over breasts and serve.

NOTES: Date: _____

RATE THIS RECIPE
○ ○ ○ ○ ○

HONEY | SOY SAUCE CHICKEN BREASTS
Marinate | Grill

	INGREDIENTS	SUBSTITUTIONS
☐ 4 – 6	skin-on chicken breasts	
☐ 3	tablespoons honey	_____
☐ 5	tablespoons soy sauce	_____
☐ 3	tablespoons extra virgin olive oil	_____
☐ 3	tablespoons chicken broth	_____
☐ ½	teaspoon onion powder	_____
☐ ½	teaspoon garlic powder	_____
☐ 1	tablespoon ground ginger	_____

1. Combine all ingredients except breasts in a re-sealable plastic bag. Mix thoroughly. Taste, adjust flavoring. Pierce each breast with a fork 6 – 8 times. Add breasts to bag. Seal bag and toss to coat breasts thoroughly. Refrigerate and marinate 3 hours. Turn occasionally to coat breasts evenly.

2. Lightly oil grill grates with no-stick cooking spray. Prepare grill for low-indirect heat. Maintain grill temperature at 275°. Place breasts on grill. Grill covered over low-indirect heat 30 – 40 minutes until done. Internal temperature should be at least 165°.

3. Platter breasts, wrap with foil and seal tightly until ready to serve.

NOTES: Date: _____

RATE THIS RECIPE
○ ○ ○ ○ ○

LEMON / BASIL CHICKEN BREASTS
Marinate | Grill

		INGREDIENTS	SUBSTITUTIONS
☐	4 – 6	skin-on chicken breasts	
☐	½	cup lemon juice	_____
☐	2	tablespoons dried basil	_____
☐	¼	teaspoon salt	_____
☐	¼	teaspoon black pepper	_____
☐	2	tablespoons Dijon mustard	_____
☐	1	tablespoon extra virgin olive oil	_____

1. Combine all ingredients except breasts in a re-sealable plastic bag. Blend thoroughly. Taste, adjust flavoring. Pierce each breast 6 – 8 times with a fork. Add breasts to bag. Seal bag and marinate in refrigerator 3 hours. Turn bag occasionally to coat breasts evenly.

2. Lightly oil grill grates with no-stick cooking spray. Prepare grill for medium-direct heat. Place breasts on grill. Grill breasts on each side until done. Internal temperature should be at least 165°.

3. Platter breasts, wrap with foil and seal tightly until ready to serve.

NOTES: Date: _____

RATE THIS RECIPE
○ ○ ○ ○ ○

LEMONADE CHICKEN BREASTS
Marinate | Grill

		INGREDIENTS	SUBSTITUTIONS
☐	4 – 6	skin-on chicken breasts	
☐	1	can (6 ounce) frozen lemonade – undiluted/thawed	_____
☐	¼	teaspoon black pepper	_____
☐	¼	teaspoon salt	_____
☐	¼	teaspoon garlic powder	_____
☐	½	teaspoon ground ginger	_____
☐	¼	teaspoon paprika	_____
☐	¼	cup soy sauce	_____

1. Combine all ingredients except breasts in a re-sealable plastic bag. Blend thoroughly. Taste, adjust flavoring. Pierce each breast 6 – 8 times with a fork. Add breasts to bag. Seal bag and marinate in refrigerator 3 hours. Turn bag occasionally to coat breasts evenly.

2. Place marinade in a saucepan, bring to boil, reduce heat and simmer 5 minutes.

3. Lightly oil grill grates with no-stick cooking spray. Prepare grill for medium-direct heat. Place breasts on grill. Grill breasts on each side until done. Baste frequently with lemonade sauce. Internal temperature should be at least 165°.

4. Platter breasts, wrap with foil and seal tightly until ready to serve.

NOTES: Date: _____

RATE THIS RECIPE
○ ○ ○ ○ ○

ORANGE JUICE / MAPLE CHICKEN BREASTS
Grill

		INGREDIENTS	SUBSTITUTIONS
☐	4 – 6	skin-on chicken breasts	
☐	⅓	cup orange juice	_____
☐	⅓	cup maple syrup	_____
☐	2	tablespoons cider vinegar	_____
☐	2	teaspoons Dijon mustard	_____
☐	½	teaspoon salt – divided	_____
☐	¾	teaspoon black pepper – divided	_____
☐	1	teaspoon dried basil	_____
☐	½	teaspoon grated orange peel	_____

1. Combine orange juice, syrup, vinegar, mustard, ¼ teaspoon salt and ¼ teaspoon black pepper in a saucepan. Bring to a boil, reduce heat and simmer until sauce is reduced to one half cup. Taste, adjust flavoring. Stir in basil and orange peel and blend thoroughly. Set aside to use as baste later.

2. Lightly oil grill grates with no-stick cooking spray. Prepare grill for medium-direct heat. Season breasts with remaining salt and pepper. Place breasts on grill. Baste liberally with orange juice sauce while grilling. Grill breasts on each side until done. Internal temperature should be at least 165°.

3. Platter breasts, wrap with foil and seal tightly until ready to serve.

NOTES: Date: _____

RATE THIS RECIPE
○ ○ ○ ○ ○

ORANGE JUICE / RUM CHICKEN BREASTS
Marinate | Grill

		INGREDIENTS	SUBSTITUTIONS
☐	4 – 6	skin-on chicken breasts	
☐	¼	cup orange juice	_____
☐	2	teaspoons rum extract	_____
☐	¼	cup soy sauce	_____
☐	2	tablespoons brown sugar	_____
☐	2	garlic cloves – minced	_____
☐	1	teaspoon ground ginger	_____
☐	½	teaspoon hot pepper sauce	_____

1. Combine all ingredients except breasts in a bowl. Blend thoroughly. Taste, adjust flavoring. Pour mixture into a re-sealable plastic bag. Pierce each breast 6 – 8 times with a fork. Add breasts to bag. Seal bag and toss to coat breasts thoroughly. Refrigerate and marinate 3 hours. Turn bag occasionally to coat breasts evenly.

2. Pour marinade from bag into a saucepan. Bring to a boil. Reduce heat and simmer 5 minutes. Set aside.

3. Lightly oil grill grates with no-stick cooking spray. Prepare grill for medium-direct heat. Place breasts on grill. Grill breasts on each side until done. Baste with marinade near end of cooking. Internal temperature should be at least 165°.

4. Serve with remaining cooked marinade.

NOTES:　　　　　　　　　　　　　　　　Date: _____

RATE THIS RECIPE
○ ○ ○ ○ ○

PINEAPPLE | BROWN SUGAR CHICKEN BREASTS
Marinate | Grill

		INGREDIENTS	SUBSTITUTIONS
☐	4 – 6	skin-on chicken breasts	
☐	2	cups pineapple juice	_____
☐	3	tablespoons brown sugar	_____
☐	3	tablespoons Worcestershire sauce	_____
☐	¼	cup soy sauce	_____
☐	1	teaspoon ground ginger	_____

1. Place all ingredients except breasts in a re-sealable plastic bag. Blend thoroughly. Taste, adjust flavoring. Pierce each breast 6 – 8 times with a fork. Add breasts to bag and coat thoroughly. Seal bag and marinate 3 hours in refrigerator. Turn bag occasionally to coat breasts evenly.

2. Lightly oil grill grates with no-stick cooking spray. Prepare grill for medium-direct heat. Place breasts on grill. Grill breasts on each side until done. Internal temperature should be at least 165°.

3. Platter breasts, wrap with foil and seal tightly until ready to serve.

NOTES: Date: _____

RATE THIS RECIPE
○ ○ ○ ○ ○

RASPBERRY CHICKEN BREASTS
Marinate | Grill

	INGREDIENTS	SUBSTITUTIONS
☐ 4 – 6	skin-on chicken breasts	
☐ ¼	cup cider vinegar	_____
☐ 2	tablespoons extra virgin olive oil	_____
☐ 2	teaspoons dried tarragon	_____
☐ ½	teaspoon black pepper	_____
☐ 1	tablespoon soy sauce	_____
☐ 1	cup concentrated raspberry juice – undiluted/thawed	_____
☐ 1	tablespoon cornstarch	_____

1. Combine vinegar, oil, tarragon, black pepper and soy sauce in a re-sealable plastic bag and blend thoroughly. Taste, adjust flavoring. Pierce each breast 6 – 8 times with a fork. Add breasts to bag, seal and marinate in refrigerator 3 hours. Turn bag occasionally to coat breasts evenly.

2. Remove breasts from bag. Pour marinade into a saucepan and bring to a boil. Reduce heat and simmer 5 minutes.

3. Lightly oil grill grates with no-stick cooking spray. Prepare grill for medium-direct heat. Place breasts on grill. Brush frequently with marinade mixture from saucepan. Grill breasts on each side until done. Internal temperature should be at least 165°.

4. Combine raspberry juice and cornstarch in a saucepan. Thicken over medium-low heat 6 – 8 minutes. Pool sauce in middle of a platter and place breasts on top of sauce.

NOTES: Date: _____

RATE THIS RECIPE
○ ○ ○ ○ ○

RASPBERRY SAUCE CHICKEN BREASTS
Grill | Flattened

		INGREDIENTS	SUBSTITUTIONS
☐	4 – 6	skin-on chicken breasts	
☐	½	teaspoon salt – divided	_____
☐	½	teaspoon black pepper – divided	_____
☐	2	cups fresh red raspberries	_____
☐	½	cup raspberry jam	_____
☐	3	tablespoons red wine vinegar	_____
☐	½	teaspoon oregano	_____

1. Place each breast between sheets of plastic wrap and gently pound flat to an even 1 – 1½ inch thickness. Sprinkle with ¼ teaspoon salt and ¼ teaspoon black pepper. Cover and set aside in refrigerator.

2. In a saucepan, combine raspberries, jam, vinegar, oregano, ¼ teaspoon salt and ¼ teaspoon black pepper. Bring to a boil. Reduce heat and simmer about 5 – 6 minutes. Mash berries with a fork and stir frequently. Cool. Strain raspberry sauce through a fine mesh strainer into a bowl. Refrigerate. Warm when ready to serve.

3. Lightly oil grill grates with no-stick cooking spray. Prepare grill for medium-direct heat. Grill flattened breasts over medium-direct heat on each side until done. Internal temperature should be at least 165°.

4. Place breasts on a platter and spoon warm raspberry sauce over breasts and serve.

NOTES: Date: _____

RATE THIS RECIPE
○ ○ ○ ○ ○

SOUR CREAM CHICKEN BREASTS
Marinate | Grill

		INGREDIENTS	SUBSTITUTIONS
☐	4 – 6	skin-on chicken breasts	
☐	3	teaspoons lemon juice	_____
☐	3	teaspoons Worcestershire sauce	_____
☐	¾	cup sour cream	_____
☐	1	teaspoon celery salt	_____
☐	½	teaspoon ground ginger	_____
☐	½	teaspoon garlic powder	_____
☐	2	cups dry bread crumbs – fine	_____
☐	2	tablespoons sage	_____
☐	1	teaspoon black pepper	_____

1. Combine lemon juice, Worcestershire, sour cream, celery salt, ginger and garlic powder in a re-sealable plastic bag. Pierce each breast 6 – 8 times with a fork. Add breasts to bag. Seal bag and toss to coat thoroughly. Marinate breasts 3 hours in refrigerator. Turn bag occasionally to coat breasts evenly.

2. Remove breasts from bag. Place bread crumbs, sage and black pepper in another re-sealable plastic bag. Mix thoroughly. Add breasts and toss to coat thoroughly.

3. Lightly oil grill grates with no-stick cooking spray. Prepare grill for medium-direct heat. Place breasts on grill. Grill breasts on each side until done. Internal temperature should be at least 165°.

4. Platter breasts, wrap with foil and seal tightly until ready to serve.

NOTES: Date: _____

RATE THIS RECIPE
○ ○ ○ ○ ○

SWEET / SOUR CHICKEN BREASTS
Marinate | Grill

		INGREDIENTS	SUBSTITUTIONS
☐	4 – 6	skin-on chicken breasts	
☐	2	cans (8 ounce) crushed pineapple – juice/meat divided	_____
☐	1	tablespoon lemon zest	_____
☐	1	cup ketchup	_____
☐	⅓	cup brown sugar – packed	_____
☐	2	tablespoons lemon juice	_____
☐	1	tablespoon cornstarch	_____

1. Drain pineapple juice from cans. In a re-sealable plastic bag, combine pineapple juice, lemon zest, ketchup, brown sugar and lemon juice. Mix thoroughly. Taste, adjust flavoring. Pierce each breast 6 – 8 times with a fork. Add breasts to bag and seal. Refrigerate and marinate 3 hours. Turn bag occasionally to coat breasts evenly.

2. Remove breasts from bag. Pour marinade into saucepan. Add pineapple and cornstarch to saucepan. Bring to a boil, reduce heat, stir and simmer 2 – 3 minutes to thicken.

3. Lightly oil grill grates with no-stick cooking spray. Prepare grill for medium-direct heat. Baste breasts with sauce several times while grilling. Grill breasts on each side until done. Internal temperature should be at least 165°.

4. Platter breasts, wrap with foil and seal tightly until ready to serve.

NOTES: Date: _____

RATE THIS RECIPE
○ ○ ○ ○ ○

TOMATO SOUP / HONEY CHICKEN BREASTS
Grill

		INGREDIENTS	SUBSTITUTIONS
☐	4 – 6	skin-on chicken breasts	
☐	1	can (10.5 ounce) tomato soup	_____
☐	¼	cup honey	_____
☐	½	teaspoon onion powder	_____
☐	½	teaspoon ground ginger	_____
☐	2	garlic cloves – minced	_____
☐	2	teaspoons dry mustard	_____

1. Combine all ingredients except breasts in a large bowl and blend thoroughly. Taste, adjust flavoring. Divide equally between two bowls. Set one bowl aside in refrigerator.

2. Lightly oil grill grates with no-stick cooking spray. Prepare grill for medium-direct heat. Turn and baste several times with tomato soap/honey mixture while grilling. Grill breasts on each side until done. Internal temperature should be at least 165°.

3. Pour set aside mixture into a saucepan and bring to a boil. Serve with breasts.

NOTES:

Date: _____

RATE THIS RECIPE
○ ○ ○ ○ ○

VINEGAR / MAPLE SYRUP CHICKEN BREASTS
Marinate | Grill

		INGREDIENTS	SUBSTITUTIONS
☐	4 – 6	skin-on chicken breasts	
☐	½	cup cider vinegar	_____
☐	¾	cup maple syrup	_____
☐	3	tablespoons Worcestershire sauce	_____
☐	1	garlic clove – minced	_____
☐	½	teaspoon ground ginger	_____

1. Combine all ingredients except breasts in a bowl and blend thoroughly. Taste, adjust flavoring. Reserve one third cup in refrigerator for basting later. Pierce each breast 6 – 8 times with a fork. Place breasts in a re-sealable plastic bag and add remaining marinade. Seal bag and toss to coat. Place in refrigerator and marinate 3 hours. Turn bag occasionally to coat breasts evenly.

2. Lightly oil grill grates with no-stick cooking spray. Prepare grill for medium-direct heat. Place breasts on grill. Turn breasts and baste with reserved marinade several times while grilling. Grill breasts on each side until done. Internal temperature should be at least 165°.

3. Platter breasts, wrap with foil and seal tightly until ready to serve.

NOTES: Date: _____

RATE THIS RECIPE
○ ○ ○ ○ ○

VINEGAR / DIJON CHICKEN BREASTS
Marinate | Grill

		INGREDIENTS	SUBSTITUTIONS
☐	4 – 6	skin-on chicken breasts	
☐	¼	cup cider vinegar	_____
☐	3	tablespoons Dijon mustard	_____
☐	3	garlic cloves – minced	_____
☐	¼	cup lime juice	_____
☐	¼	cup lemon juice	_____
☐	½	cup brown sugar – packed	_____
☐	¼	teaspoon salt	_____
☐	¼	teaspoon black pepper	_____
☐	⅓	cup extra virgin olive oil	_____

1. Place all ingredients except breasts and oil in a re-sealable plastic bag and blend thoroughly. Add in oil and blend thoroughly. Taste, adjust flavoring. Pierce each breast 6 – 8 times with a fork. Add breasts to bag. Seal bag and marinate breasts in refrigerator 3 hours. Turn bag occasionally to coat breasts evenly.

2. Lightly oil grill grates with no-stick cooking spray. Preheat grill for medium-direct heat. Grill breasts on each side until done. Internal temperature should be at least 165°.

3. Platter breasts, wrap with foil and seal tightly until ready to serve.

NOTES:

Date: _____

RATE THIS RECIPE
○ ○ ○ ○ ○

VINEGAR / WHITE SUGAR CHICKEN BREASTS

Marinate | Grill

	INGREDIENTS	SUBSTITUTIONS
☐ 4 – 6	skin-on chicken breasts	
☐ ½	cup cider vinegar	_____
☐ ½	cup white sugar	_____
☐ ¼	teaspoon salt	_____
☐ ¼	teaspoon black pepper	_____
☐ ⅓	cup ketchup	_____
☐ ½	teaspoon dry mustard	_____
☐ ½	teaspoon paprika	_____
☐ ½	teaspoon curry powder	_____
☐ ¼	teaspoon garlic salt	_____
☐ 1	tablespoon Worcestershire sauce	_____

1. Combine all ingredients except breasts in a re-sealable plastic bag. Taste, adjust flavoring. Pierce each breast 6 – 8 times with a fork. Add breasts to bag. Seal and marinate in refrigerator 3 hours. Turn bag occasionally to coat breasts evenly.

2. Lightly oil grill grates with no-stick cooking spray. Prepare grill for medium-direct heat. Place breasts on grill. Grill breasts on each side until done. Internal temperature should be at least 165°.

3. Platter breasts, wrap with foil and seal tightly until ready to serve.

NOTES: Date: _____

RATE THIS RECIPE
○ ○ ○ ○ ○

VINEGAR | KETCHUP CHICKEN BREASTS
Marinate | Grill

	INGREDIENTS	SUBSTITUTIONS
☐ 4 – 6	skin-on chicken breasts	
☐ 6	tablespoons cider vinegar	_____
☐ 2	tablespoons ketchup	_____
☐ 3	tablespoons extra virgin olive oil	_____
☐ 2	garlic cloves – minced	_____
☐ ½	teaspoon liquid smoke	_____
☐ ½	teaspoon paprika	_____
☐ ½	teaspoon dried oregano	_____
☐ ½	teaspoon hot pepper sauce	_____
☐ ½	teaspoon Worcestershire sauce	_____

1. Combine all ingredients except breasts in a re-sealable plastic bag. Mix thoroughly. Taste, adjust flavoring. Pierce each breast 6 – 8 times with a fork. Add breasts to bag. Seal bag and toss to coat breasts thoroughly. Refrigerate and marinate 3 hours. Turn occasionally to coat breasts evenly.

2. Lightly oil grill grates with no-stick cooking spray. Prepare grill for low-indirect heat. Place breasts on grill. Grill breasts covered until done. Internal temperature should be at least 165°. Maintain grill temperature at 275°.

3. Platter breasts, wrap with foil and seal tightly until ready to serve.

NOTES: Date: _____

RATE THIS RECIPE
○ ○ ○ ○ ○

NOTES

OVEN BAKED CHICKEN BREASTS

Take recommendations about operating a safe kitchen seriously. During one particularly memorable visit with my son's family, I was using their open flame gas stove to cook for my grandchildren. I was wearing a robe with a fine nap, and as I was sautéing onions in a skillet, flames shot up the sleeve! I got the robe off quickly, bunched it in a pile on the floor and smothered the flames. I was lucky I wasn't seriously injured. Instead, I was just a bit chilly.

Also, I burned myself more than a couple of times by grabbing the handle of my cast-iron skillet after it had been in a hot oven. I learned, rather slowly, to make oven mitts my constant cooking companions. Learn from my mistakes and use those oven mitts! Stay safe. Nothing ruins a cooking adventure faster than a fire, a cut or a burn.

ARTICHOKE CHICKEN BREASTS

Oven

		INGREDIENTS	SUBSTITUTIONS
☐	4 – 6	skin-on chicken breasts	_____
☐	¼	teaspoon salt	_____
☐	¼	teaspoon black pepper	_____
☐	½	cup all-purpose flour	_____
☐	½	teaspoon ground ginger	_____
☐	1	tablespoon butter	_____
☐	1	tablespoon extra virgin olive oil	_____
☐	8	ounces mushrooms – sliced	_____
☐	2	jars (7 ounce) artichoke hearts – quartered/drained	_____
☐	1	tomato – diced	_____
☐	1	can (2.25 ounce) ripe olives – sliced	_____
☐	¼	cup chicken broth	_____
☐	¼	cup lemon juice	_____
☐	¼	cup white wine	_____

1. Combine salt, pepper, flour and ginger in a re-sealable plastic bag. Add breasts and toss to coat thoroughly.

2. Heat butter and oil over medium heat in a large oven-proof skillet. Cook breasts until golden brown. Set aside.

3. Add mushrooms to skillet and sauté 2 minutes. Add remaining ingredients including breasts and bring to a boil, reduce heat and simmer until slightly thickened.

3. Place oven rack in middle position. Preheat oven to 350°. Cover skillet with aluminum foil and transfer to oven. Bake 30 – 40 minutes until done. Internal temperature should be at least 165°.

4. Platter breasts, wrap with foil and seal tightly until ready to serve.

NOTES: Date: _____

RATE THIS RECIPE
○ ○ ○ ○ ○

BLUE CHEESE CHICKEN BREASTS
Oven | Flattened

	INGREDIENTS	SUBSTITUTIONS
☐ 4 – 6	skin-on chicken breasts	_____
☐ ¾	stick butter	_____
☐ 1	cup blue cheese – crumbled	_____
☐ ¼	teaspoon salt	_____
☐ ¼	teaspoon black pepper	_____
☐ 2	tablespoons extra virgin olive oil	_____
☐ ½	cup bread crumbs	_____

1. Place each breast between sheets of plastic wrap and gently pound flat to an even ⅓ – ½ inch thickness.

2. Cover a large baking sheet with aluminum foil. Spray with no-stick cooking spray. Place breasts on sheet. Divide butter into equal portions and position butter in center of each breast. Spread cheese equally over middle area of breasts. Season with salt and pepper.

3. Roll breasts tightly. Seal breasts with toothpicks to secure ingredients inside. Brush breast exterior with oil and add bread crumbs to top and sides of rolled breast pieces.

4. Place oven rack in middle position. Preheat oven to 350°. Cook breasts covered 30 – 40 minutes. Internal temperature should be at least 165°.

NOTES:

Date: _____

RATE THIS RECIPE
○ ○ ○ ○ ○

BLUE CHEESE / BACON CHICKEN BREASTS
Oven

	INGREDIENTS	SUBSTITUTIONS
☐ 4 – 6	skin-on chicken breasts	
☐ 3	slices bacon	_____
☐ 1	stick butter	_____
☐ ½	cup blue cheese – crumbled	_____
☐ 1	scallion – white only/minced	_____
☐ ½	teaspoon salt – divided	_____
☐ ½	teaspoon black pepper – divided	_____
☐ 2 – 3	ounces butter	_____

1. Cook bacon in a saucepan over medium-high heat until crisp. Drain on paper towel. Crumble. Melt 1 stick butter in a saucepan. Place bacon, butter, blue cheese, scallion, ¼ teaspoon salt and ¼ teaspoon black pepper in a bowl and mix thoroughly.

2. Loosen breast skins with broad blunt knife. Do not break skin. Spoon equal amounts of butter mixture under skin of each breast. Smooth mixture under skin. Secure skin flaps with toothpicks.

3. Place oven rack in middle position. Preheat oven to 350°. Place breasts skin-side up in large greased baking pan. Sprinkle with ¼ teaspoon salt and ¼ teaspoon black pepper. Bake uncovered in oven 20 minutes.

4. Remove breasts from oven and baste with pan juices. Baste with ½ ounce butter on each breast. Bake 10 – 20 minutes more until done. Internal temperature should be at least 165°.

5. Platter breasts, wrap with foil and seal tightly until ready to serve.

NOTES: Date: _____

RATE THIS RECIPE
○ ○ ○ ○ ○

GREEN OLIVE CHICKEN BREASTS
Oven

	INGREDIENTS	SUBSTITUTIONS
☐ 4 – 6	skinless chicken breasts	
☐ 2	tablespoons butter	_____
☐ 2	tablespoons garlic – minced	_____
☐ ¼	cup lemon juice	_____
☐ ½	teaspoon dried tarragon	_____
☐ 20	pitted green olives	_____
☐ ¼	teaspoon salt	_____
☐ ½	teaspoon black pepper	_____

1. Heat butter in an oven-proof skillet over medium heat. Add breasts and cook until golden brown. Add garlic, lemon juice, tarragon and olives to skillet. Mix thoroughly.

2. Place oven rack in middle position. Preheat oven to 350°. Season breasts with salt and black pepper. Place skillet in oven and bake breasts 30 – 40 minutes until done. Internal temperature should be at least 165°.

NOTES: Date: _____

RATE THIS RECIPE
○ ○ ○ ○ ○

HONEY CHICKEN BREASTS
Oven

		INGREDIENTS	SUBSTITUTIONS
☐	4 – 6	skin-on chicken breasts	
☐	½	cup honey	_____
☐	¼	cup pineapple juice	_____
☐	1	tablespoon Dijon mustard	_____
☐	1	teaspoon curry powder	_____
☐	½	teaspoon ground ginger	_____
☐	¼	teaspoon salt	_____
☐	4	tablespoons butter	_____

1. Combine honey, pineapple juice, mustard, curry powder, ginger and salt in a bowl.

2. Melt butter in a large baking dish. Add breasts and turn to coat breasts thoroughly with butter. Pour honey mixture over breasts and coat well.

3. Place oven rack in middle position. Preheat oven to 350°. Bake 20 minutes covered. Turn breasts and continue baking uncovered 10 – 20 minutes until done. Baste with dish juices. Internal temperature should be at least 165°.

4. Platter breasts, wrap with foil and seal tightly until ready to serve.

NOTES: Date: _____

RATE THIS RECIPE
○ ○ ○ ○ ○

HONEY / PINEAPPLE CHICKEN BREASTS

Marinate | Oven

		INGREDIENTS	SUBSTITUTIONS
☐	4 – 6	skin-on chicken breasts	
☐	2	tablespoons Worcestershire sauce	_____
☐	¾	cup white wine	_____
☐	¼	cup chicken broth	_____
☐	1	teaspoon dried tarragon	_____
☐	2	cans (8 ounce) unsweetened pineapple	_____
☐	¼	cup honey	_____

1. Combine Worcestershire, wine, broth and tarragon in a re-sealable plastic bag and blend thoroughly. Pierce each breast 6 – 8 times with a fork. Add breasts to bag and marinate in refrigerator 3 hours. Turn bag occasionally to coat breasts evenly.

2. Place oven rack in middle position. Preheat oven to 350°. Drain marinade from bag to a saucepan.

3. Cover a large baking sheet with aluminum foil and spray lightly with no-stick cooking spray. Place breasts on sheet and distribute pineapple equally over breasts. Bake breasts uncovered 30 – 40 minutes until done. Internal temperature should be at least 165°.

4. Platter breasts, wrap with foil and seal tightly until ready to serve.

5. Add honey to marinade in saucepan. Bring to boil, reduce heat and simmer 5 minutes. Spoon over breasts.

NOTES: Date: _____

RATE THIS RECIPE
○ ○ ○ ○ ○

LEMON CHICKEN BREASTS
Oven

	INGREDIENTS	SUBSTITUTIONS
☐ 4 – 6	skin-on chicken breasts	
☐ 3	tablespoons extra virgin olive oil – divided	_____
☐ 3	tablespoons garlic cloves – minced	_____
☐ 3	tablespoons onion – chopped	_____
☐ ¼	cup dry white wine	_____
☐ 1	tablespoon lemon zest	_____
☐ 2	tablespoons lemon juice	_____
☐ 2	teaspoons dried oregano	_____
☐ 1	teaspoon dried thyme	_____
☐ ½	teaspoon rosemary	_____
☐ ½	teaspoon ground ginger	_____
☐ ¼	teaspoon salt	_____
☐ ½	teaspoon black pepper	_____
☐ 2	lemons – sliced	_____

1. Heat 2 tablespoons oil in a skillet over medium heat. Sauté garlic and onion until onions are wilted and translucent.

2. Combine garlic, onion, wine, lemon zest, lemon juice, oregano, thyme, rosemary and ginger in a bowl. Mix thoroughly. Pour mixture into a baking dish. Place breasts on top of mixture. Brush breasts with 1 tablespoon oil. Season with salt and pepper. Place sliced lemon over and around breasts.

3. Place oven rack in middle position. Preheat oven to 350°. Bake breasts 30 – 40 minutes until done. Internal temperature should be at least 165°.

NOTES: Date: _____

RATE THIS RECIPE
○ ○ ○ ○ ○

LEMON CRISP CHICKEN BREASTS
Oven

		INGREDIENTS	SUBSTITUTIONS
☐	4 – 6	skin-on chicken breasts	
☐	1	large lemon – grated/peeled/sliced/juiced	_____
☐	3	tablespoons butter	_____
☐	4	garlic cloves – chopped	_____
☐	½	teaspoon salt – divided	_____
☐	½	teaspoon black pepper – divided	_____
☐	8	teaspoons butter – divided	_____

1. Grate lemon peel to obtain 4 tablespoons zest. Squeeze lemon to obtain ¼ cup lemon juice. Slice lemon into 8 thin slices. Set aside.

2. Melt butter in a saucepan. Purée grated lemon zest, 2 teaspoons lemon juice, garlic, ¼ teaspoon salt, ¼ teaspoon black pepper and 2 tablespoons butter in a blender. Pour into a bowl. Add lemon slices to bowl and let rest 10 minutes.

3. Loosen breasts skins with broad blunt knife. Insert a lemon slice under skin of each breasts. Spoon lemon mixture under skin onto lemon slices. Do not break skin. Secure skin flaps with toothpicks.

4. Place oven rack in middle position. Preheat oven to 350°. Place breasts in large greased baking dish. Sprinkle remaining lemon juice over breasts. Sprinkle with ¼ teaspoon salt and ¼ teaspoon black pepper. Place 1 teaspoon butter on each breasts. Bake uncovered 20 minutes.

5. Remove breasts from oven, turn and baste with dish juices. Bake additional 10 – 20 minutes until done. Internal temperature should be at least 165°.

NOTES: Date: _____

RATE THIS RECIPE
○ ○ ○ ○ ○

MUSHROOM CHICKEN BREASTS
Oven

	INGREDIENTS	SUBSTITUTIONS
☐ 4 – 6	skin-on chicken breasts	
☐ 1	can (10.75 ounce) cream of mushroom soup	_____
☐ 1	cup milk	_____
☐ ½	teaspoon onion powder	_____
☐ 1	cup dry bread crumbs	_____
☐ ½	teaspoon paprika	_____
☐ ¼	cup all-purpose flour	_____
☐ ¼	teaspoon salt	_____
☐ ¼	teaspoon black pepper	_____
☐ ½	stick butter	_____
☐ 1	teaspoon cornstarch	_____
☐ 1	can (4 ounce) sliced mushrooms	_____

1. Place oven rack in middle position. Preheat oven to 350°.

2. Combine soup, milk and onion powder in a medium bowl and mix well. Place bread crumbs, paprika, flour, salt and black pepper in a re-sealable plastic bag. Wet breasts in mushroom soup mixture and add to bag. Seal bag and shake to thoroughly coat breasts. Reserve soup mixture and set aside.

3. Melt butter in a small saucepan. Place breasts on a baking sheet. Distribute melted butter evenly over breasts. Bake 30 – 40 minutes until done. Internal temperature should be at least 165°.

4. Bring remaining soup mixture to a near boil in a saucepan. Add cornstarch and mushrooms and thicken. Serve with breasts.

NOTES: Date: _____

RATE THIS RECIPE
○ ○ ○ ○ ○

MUSHROOM / SOUR CREAM CHICKEN BREASTS
Oven

	INGREDIENTS	SUBSTITUTIONS
☐ 4 – 6	skin-on chicken breasts	
☐ 1	tablespoon extra virgin olive oil	_____
☐ ¼	teaspoon salt	_____
☐ ¼	teaspoon black pepper	_____
☐ ¼	teaspoon sage	_____
☐ ½	teaspoon paprika	_____
☐ 1	can (10.75 ounce) cream of mushroom soup	_____
☐ 1	can (4 ounce) sliced mushrooms	_____
☐ 1	package (1 ounce) dry onion soup mix	_____
☐ 1	cup sour cream	_____
☐ ½	teaspoon ground ginger	_____
☐ 1	tablespoon lemon juice	_____
☐ 1	teaspoon dried dill weed	_____

1. Heat oil in a skillet over medium heat. Cook breasts until golden brown.

2. Place oven rack in middle position. Preheat oven to 350°. Place breasts in a large greased baking dish. Combine salt, pepper, sage and paprika in a bowl. Mix well. Sprinkle over breasts.

3. Combine soup, mushrooms, onion soup mix, sour cream, ginger, lemon juice and dill weed in a bowl and blend together thoroughly. Taste, adjust flavoring. Pour soup mixture over breasts.

4. Place breasts in oven uncovered and cook 30 – 40 minutes until done. Internal temperature should be at least 165°.

NOTES: Date: _____

RATE THIS RECIPE
○ ○ ○ ○ ○

ORANGE CHICKEN BREASTS
Oven

		INGREDIENTS	SUBSTITUTIONS
☐	4 – 6	skin-on chicken breasts	
☐	7	tablespoons butter – divided	_____
☐	3	tablespoons extra virgin olive oil	_____
☐	½	teaspoon salt – divided	_____
☐	½	teaspoon black pepper – divided	_____
☐	½	cup orange juice	_____
☐	1	can (14 ounce) chicken broth	_____
☐	2	teaspoons dried tarragon	_____

1. Place 3 tablespoons butter and oil in a large skillet. Sprinkle ¼ teaspoon salt and ¼ teaspoon black pepper over breasts. Cook breasts in skillet over medium heat until golden brown.

2. Place oven rack in middle position. Preheat oven to 350°. Place skillet in oven. Cook breasts 10 –15 minutes.

3. Combine orange juice, chicken broth and tarragon in a bowl. Mix thoroughly. Pour mixture over breasts. Return skillet to oven. Cook until liquid is reduced by about three quarters, approximately 20 – 30 minutes and breasts are done. Internal temperature should be at least 165°.

4. Melt 4 tablespoons butter in a saucepan. Distribute butter equally over breasts. Remove breasts and platter. Taste sauce in skillet, adjust flavoring with ¼ teaspoon salt and ¼ teaspoon black pepper. Spoon sauce over breasts and serve.

NOTES: Date: _____

RATE THIS RECIPE
○ ○ ○ ○ ○

PARMESAN CHICKEN BREASTS
Oven

	INGREDIENTS	SUBSTITUTIONS
☐ 4 – 6	skin-on chicken breasts	_____
☐ 1	cup Parmesan cheese	_____
☐ 1	cup dry bread crumbs – fine	_____
☐ 1	tablespoon oregano	_____
☐ 3	large eggs – beaten	_____
☐ ⅓	cup Italian salad dressing	_____
☐ 4 – 6	tablespoons butter	_____

1. Combine cheese, bread crumbs and oregano in a re-sealable plastic bag. Whisk eggs in a bowl. Dip breasts into eggs and add breasts to bag and toss to coat evenly.

2. Cover a large baking sheet with aluminum foil and spray with no-stick cooking spray. Place breasts on sheet. Drizzle with salad dressing. Place 1 tablespoon butter on each breast.

3. Place oven rack in middle position. Preheat oven to 350°. Bake covered 30 – 40 minutes until done. Internal temperature should be at least 165°.

4. Platter breasts, wrap with foil and seal tightly until ready to serve.

NOTES: Date: _____

RATE THIS RECIPE
○ ○ ○ ○ ○

PEACH GLAZED CHICKEN BREASTS
Oven

		INGREDIENTS	SUBSTITUTIONS
☐	4 – 6	skin-on chicken breasts	
☐	3	tablespoons butter	_____
☐	¼	teaspoon salt	_____
☐	¼	teaspoon black pepper	_____
☐	⅔	cup peach preserves	_____
☐	1	tablespoon Dijon mustard	_____
☐	1	teaspoon cider vinegar	_____
☐	¼	teaspoon dried thyme	_____

1. Place oven rack in middle position. Preheat oven to 350°. Cover a large baking sheet with aluminum foil. Spray foil with no-stick cooking spray. Place breasts on prepared baking sheet.

2. Melt butter in a small saucepan. Brush breasts with melted butter. Season breasts with salt and pepper. Bake covered 20 minutes.

3. Combine all others ingredients in a bowl and stir to mix thoroughly. Coat breasts thoroughly with mixture. Bake an additional 15 – 25 minutes covered until done. Internal temperature should be at least 165°.

4. Platter breasts, wrap with foil and seal tightly until ready to serve.

NOTES: Date: _____

RATE THIS RECIPE
○ ○ ○ ○ ○

PINEAPPLE CHICKEN BREASTS
Oven

		INGREDIENTS	SUBSTITUTIONS
☐	4 – 6	skin-on chicken breasts	
☐	¼	teaspoon salt	_____
☐	¼	teaspoon black pepper	_____
☐	1	teaspoon dried crushed rosemary	_____
☐	10	scallions – white only/thinly sliced	_____
☐	2	teaspoons candied ginger – finely chopped	_____
☐	1	cup pineapple juice	_____
☐	4 – 6	slices pineapples – halved	_____

1. Combine salt, black pepper and rosemary in a bowl and mix thoroughly as a rub. Massage breasts thoroughly with rub.

2. Cover a large baking sheet with aluminum foil and spray with no-stick cooking spray. Place breasts on sheet. Sprinkle with scallions. Combine candied ginger and pineapple juice in a bowl and mix thoroughly. Distribute evenly over breasts.

3. Place oven rack in middle position. Preheat oven to 350°. Bake breasts 30 – 40 minutes until done. Baste with juices several times. Internal temperature should be at least 165°. About 6 – 8 minutes before breasts are done, place pineapple slices on breasts.

4. Platter breasts, wrap with foil and seal tightly until ready to serve.

NOTES: Date: _____

RATE THIS RECIPE
○ ○ ○ ○ ○

SOUR CREAM CHICKEN BREASTS
Oven

		INGREDIENTS	SUBSTITUTIONS
☐	4 – 6	skin-on chicken breasts	
☐	½	cup all-purpose flour	_____
☐	2	teaspoons salt	_____
☐	¼	teaspoon black pepper	_____
☐	½	stick butter	_____
☐	½	can (14 ounce) chicken broth	_____
☐	8	ounces fresh mushrooms – sliced	_____
☐	1	cup sour cream	_____
☐	1½	teaspoons paprika	_____

1. In a re-sealable plastic bag, combine flour, salt and black pepper. Add breasts and toss to coat thoroughly.

2. Melt butter in a large skillet over medium heat and cook breasts until golden brown. Remove breasts and set aside.

3. Add broth, mushrooms, sour cream and paprika to skillet and mix thoroughly. Return breasts to skillet and coat thoroughly.

4. Place oven rack in middle position. Preheat oven to 350°. Cover skillet, place in oven and bake 30 – 40 minutes until breasts are done. Internal temperature should be at least 165°.

5. Platter breasts, wrap with foil and seal tightly until ready to serve.

NOTES: Date: _____

RATE THIS RECIPE
○ ○ ○ ○ ○

SOUR CREAM / SALSA CHICKEN BREASTS
Oven

		INGREDIENTS	SUBSTITUTIONS
☐	4 – 6	skin-on chicken breasts	
☐	1	package (1.25 ounce) taco season mix	_____
☐	1	cup salsa	_____
☐	¼	cup sour cream	_____

1. Place oven rack in middle position. Preheat oven to 350°. Line a baking dish with aluminum foil and spray lightly with no-stick cooking spray. Place breasts in dish. Distribute taco mix equally over breasts. Distribute salsa equally over breasts.

2. Bake covered 30 – 40 minutes until done. Internal temperature should be at least 165°. Remove breasts from baking dish and set aside.

3. Stir sour cream into baking dish. Mix thoroughly. Return breasts to dish and coat thoroughly.

4. Platter breasts, wrap with foil and seal tightly until ready to serve.

NOTES:	Date: _____

RATE THIS RECIPE
○ ○ ○ ○ ○

The **RASPBERRY SAUCE CHICKEN BREASTS** recipe on page 45 is near and dear to my heart.

The recipe calls for flattened breasts. I always in the past had mixed results with the flattening process. When I prepared this recipe, I had the bright idea of placing a piece of board over the breasts and pounding the board with the mallet instead of the breasts directly. They flattened beautifully!

This was a revelation for me, and has made preparing flattened breasts much more productive and enjoyable.

SPINACH STUFFED CHICKEN BREASTS
Oven | Flattened

		INGREDIENTS	SUBSTITUTIONS
☐	4 – 6	skin-on chicken breasts	
☐	3	slices bacon	_____
☐	1	medium onion – chopped	_____
☐	1	package (10 ounce) frozen spinach – thawed/patted dry	_____
☐	1	egg – beaten	_____
☐	16	ounces ricotta cheese	_____
☐	½	teaspoon garlic powder	_____
☐	½	teaspoon dried leaf oregano	_____
☐	½	teaspoon dried leaf basil	_____
☐	¼	teaspoon black pepper	_____
☐	½	teaspoon nutmeg	_____
☐	3	tablespoons butter	_____

1. Cook bacon in a skillet over medium heat until crisp. Remove from skillet and crumble. Set aside. Add onion to skillet. Sauté onion in bacon drippings over medium heat until wilted and translucent.

2. Squeeze dry spinach with paper toweling. In a large bowl, combine bacon, onion, spinach, egg, cheese, garlic powder, oregano, basil, black pepper and nutmeg and mix thoroughly.

3. Place each breast between sheets of plastic wrap and gently pound flat to an even ⅓ – ½ inch thickness. Place approximately 2 tablespoons spinach-cheese filling on each breast and roll up. Fasten with toothpicks.

4. Cover a large baking sheet with aluminum foil spray with no-stick cooking spray. Place breasts in one layer on baking sheet. Melt butter in small saucepan and drizzle over breasts.

5. Place oven rack in middle position. Preheat oven to 350°. Bake breasts covered 20 – 30 minutes until done. Internal temperature should be at least 165°.

6. Platter breasts, wrap with foil and seal tightly until ready to serve.

NOTES: Date: _____

RATE THIS RECIPE
○ ○ ○ ○ ○

NOTES

NOTES

STOVE TOP
CHICKEN BREASTS

CELERY / GARLIC CHICKEN BREASTS
Stove Top

	INGREDIENTS	SUBSTITUTIONS
☐ 4 – 6	skin-on chicken breasts	
☐ 2	tablespoons extra virgin olive oil	_____
☐ ¼	teaspoon salt	_____
☐ 1	teaspoon black pepper	_____
☐ 8	garlic cloves – halved	_____
☐ 3	celery stalks – 1-inch pieces	_____
☐ ½	teaspoon onion powder	_____
☐ ½	teaspoon ground ginger	_____
☐ 1	cup dry white wine	_____
☐ 1	cup water	_____

1. Pour oil into a large skillet over medium-high heat. Sprinkle breasts with salt and pepper. Cook breasts until golden brown. Transfer to a plate.

2. Place garlic, celery, onion powder and ginger in the skillet and cook 4 – 6 minutes. Stir frequently.

3. Add wine and bring to boil, uncovered, until liquid is reduced by one half. Taste, adjust flavoring. Stir frequently.

4. Add water and reduce heat. Return breasts to skillet and simmer slightly covered until done. Internal temperature should be at least 165°.

NOTES: Date: _____

RATE THIS RECIPE
○ ○ ○ ○ ○

CHEDDAR CHEESE / WHITE WINE CHICKEN BREASTS
Stove Top

	INGREDIENTS	SUBSTITUTIONS
☐ 4 – 6	skin-on chicken breasts	_____
☐ 2	tablespoons extra virgin olive oil	_____
☐ ¼	stick butter	_____
☐ 2	medium onions – diced	_____
☐ 2	large green bell peppers – chopped	_____
☐ 1	teaspoon black pepper	_____
☐ 1	teaspoon cayenne pepper	_____
☐ ¼	teaspoon salt	_____
☐ ½	teaspoon ground ginger	_____
☐ 1	garlic clove – chopped	_____
☐ 2	cans (6 ounce) tomato paste	_____
☐ ½	cup cheddar cheese – grated	_____
☐ 1	cup white wine	_____
☐ 2	cups cooked white rice	_____

1. Place oil, butter, onions, bell pepper and black pepper in a large skillet over medium-low heat and sauté until onions are wilted and translucent.

2. Pierce each breast with fork 6 – 8 times. Add breasts and remaining ingredients to skillet.

3. Cover and simmer on low until breasts are done. Turn once while simmering. Internal temperature should be at least 165°.

4. Serve with cooked rice.

NOTES: Date: _____

RATE THIS RECIPE
○ ○ ○ ○ ○

The **CHEDDAR CHEESE / WHITE WINE CHICKEN BREASTS** recipe on the opposite page is a great example of how substitution experimentation can result in a superb recipe.

This particular recipe comes from a dear aunt of mine. Though most of the ingredients that you find here were in her recipe, the ingredient amounts were significantly different. When preparing the marinade, I increased the amount of onion, bell pepper and tomato paste and decreased the garlic. I also added a bit of kick with the cayenne pepper which was not one of the original ingredients.

This is one of those recipes with a lot of room for experimentation. Next time I cook this, I'm sure I will make one or two alterations just to taste what happens.

CILANTRO / CREAM SAUCE CHICKEN BREASTS
Stove Top

		INGREDIENTS	SUBSTITUTIONS
☐	4 – 6	skin-on chicken breasts	
☐	¼	teaspoon salt	_____
☐	½	teaspoon black pepper	_____
☐	1	teaspoon Cajun seasoning – divided	_____
☐	2	tablespoons extra virgin olive oil	_____
☐	6	scallions – white only/sliced	_____
☐	½	red bell pepper – sliced	_____
☐	1	can (14 ounce) chicken broth	_____
☐	¼	cup dry white wine	_____
☐	½	cup half-and-half	_____
☐	1	tablespoon butter	_____
☐	½	cup cherry tomatoes – halved	_____
☐	½	cup cilantro – no stems/chopped	_____

1. Sprinkle breasts with salt and black pepper and ½ teaspoon Cajun seasoning.

2. Heat oil in a large skillet over medium-high heat. Add breasts. Cook, turning several times, until breasts are done. Internal temperature should be at least 165°. Platter breasts, wrap with foil and seal tightly.

3. Add scallions and bell pepper to skillet. Cook, stirring, 1 – 2 minutes. Add chicken broth and wine. Bring to a boil. Reduce heat and simmer until reduced to about half a cup.

4. Add half-and-half and butter, and continue simmering on low 4 – 5 minutes to reduce mixture additionally. Add tomatoes, cilantro and remaining ½ teaspoon Cajun seasoning. Mix thoroughly. Taste, adjust flavoring. Simmer 2 – 3 minutes.

5. Return breasts to skillet, cover and heat through.

NOTES: Date: _____

RATE THIS RECIPE
○ ○ ○ ○ ○

COCONUT / SPINACH CHICKEN BREASTS
Stove Top

	INGREDIENTS	SUBSTITUTIONS
☐ 4 – 6	skin-on chicken breasts	
☐ ¼	tablespoon butter	_____
☐ 1	large onion – diced	_____
☐ 1	package (10 ounce) frozen spinach – thawed/patted dry	_____
☐ ½	cup coconut milk	_____
☐ ¼	teaspoon garlic powder	_____
☐ ¼	teaspoon ground ginger	_____
☐ ¼	teaspoon salt	_____
☐ ¼	teaspoon black pepper	_____

1. Melt butter in a large skillet over medium heat. Add onion and sauté until wilted and translucent.

2. Add breasts to skillet and cook until done. Turn frequently. Internal temperature should be at least 165°.

3. Squeeze spinach dry with paper toweling. Mix spinach, coconut milk, garlic powder and ginger in a saucepan and warm but do not boil. Season with salt and pepper. Taste, adjust flavoring.

4. Pour mixture over breasts and serve.

NOTES: Date: _____

RATE THIS RECIPE
○ ○ ○ ○ ○

CORN / JALAPEÑO CHICKEN BREASTS
Stove Top

		INGREDIENTS	SUBSTITUTIONS
☐	4 – 6	skin-on chicken breasts	_____
☐	2	tablespoons extra virgin olive oil	_____
☐	¼	teaspoon salt	_____
☐	½	teaspoon black pepper	_____
☐	1	medium onion – chopped	_____
☐	2	jalapeño peppers – seeded/chopped	_____
☐	8	garlic cloves – chopped	_____
☐	2	celery stalks – chopped	_____
☐	2	medium tomatoes – diced	_____
☐	2	cans (8.75 ounce) whole kernel corn	_____
☐	3	tablespoons lime juice	_____
☐	1	tablespoon lime zest	_____
☐	2	tablespoons chili powder	_____
☐	2	cups cooked white rice	_____

1. Add oil to a large skillet over medium-high heat. Season breasts with salt and pepper. Cook breasts until golden brown. Set aside.

2. Add chopped onion, jalapeño peppers, garlic and celery to skillet. Sauté until onion is wilted and translucent. Add tomatoes, corn, lime juice, lime zest, and chili powder. Blend thoroughly.

3. Arrange breasts on top of ingredients. Cover and simmer until breasts are done. Internal temperature should be at least 165°.

4. Serve with cooked rice.

NOTES: Date: _____

RATE THIS RECIPE
○ ○ ○ ○ ○

CRANBERRIES / ORANGE CHICKEN BREASTS

Stove Top

	INGREDIENTS	SUBSTITUTIONS
☐ 4 – 6	skin-on chicken breasts	
☐ ½	cup all-purpose flour	_____
☐ ¼	teaspoon salt	_____
☐ ½	teaspoon black pepper	_____
☐ 2	tablespoons extra virgin olive oil	_____
☐ ¾	cup orange juice	_____
☐ ¼	cup Cointreau	_____
☐ ½	cup dried cranberries – chopped	_____
☐ ½	teaspoon ground ginger	_____
☐ 2	scallions – white only/sliced	_____
☐ 2	cups cooked white rice	_____

1. Combine flour, salt and black pepper in a re-sealable plastic bag. Add breasts and coat thoroughly.

2. Heat oil over medium-low heat in a skillet. Cook breasts until golden brown.

3. Combine orange juice, Cointreau, cranberries and ginger in a bowl. Blend thoroughly and pour over breasts. Cover skillet and cook over low heat 20 minutes. Stir in scallions and simmer until scallions and breasts are done. Internal temperature should be at least 165°.

4. Platter breasts, wrap with foil and seal tightly until ready to serve. Serve with cooked rice.

NOTES: Date: _____

RATE THIS RECIPE
○ ○ ○ ○ ○

CRANBERRY / SOUR CREAM CHICKEN BREASTS
Stove Top

	INGREDIENTS	SUBSTITUTIONS
☐ 4 – 6	skin-on chicken breasts	
☐ ½	cup sweetened dried cranberries	_____
☐ ½	cup apple juice	_____
☐ ½	cup chicken broth	_____
☐ ¼	cup all-purpose flour	_____
☐ ¼	teaspoon salt	_____
☐ ½	teaspoon black pepper	_____
☐ ½	teaspoon ground ginger	_____
☐ 2	tablespoons extra virgin olive oil	_____
☐ 1	tablespoon Dijon mustard	_____
☐ ½	cup sour cream (garnish)	_____

1. Combine cranberries, apple juice and broth in a small bowl and mix thoroughly. Set aside.

2. Place flour, salt, black pepper and ginger in a re-sealable plastic bag. Add breasts and coat thoroughly.

3. Place oil in skillet over medium-high heat. Cook breasts until golden brown and set aside.

4. Add cranberry mixture to skillet. Reduce heat to simmer and scrape brown bits from bottom of pan. Add mustard and blend thoroughly.

5. Return breasts to skillet. Simmer until breasts are done. Internal temperature should be at least 165°. Spoon sauce over breasts, place a dollop of sour cream on top of each breast and serve.

NOTES: Date: _____

RATE THIS RECIPE
○ ○ ○ ○ ○

CREAM / BRANDY CHICKEN BREASTS
Stove Top

	INGREDIENTS	SUBSTITUTIONS
☐ 4 – 6	skin-on chicken breasts	
☐ 2	tablespoons butter	_____
☐ 1	scallion – white only/chopped	_____
☐ 3	apples – peeled/cored/quartered	_____
☐ ¾	cup dry white wine – divided	_____
☐ ¼	teaspoon salt	_____
☐ ⅛	teaspoon black pepper	_____
☐ ¼	teaspoon ground nutmeg	_____
☐ ½	teaspoon ground ginger	_____
☐ 1	cup half-and-half	_____
☐ 1	teaspoon all-purpose flour	_____
☐ 3	tablespoons brandy	_____
☐ 2	egg yolks	_____

1. In a large heavy skillet, melt butter over medium heat. Add scallion and sauté until scallion is limp. Add breasts and cook until golden brown. Add apple. Cook over medium-low heat uncovered, stirring occasionally, about 5 minutes. Add ¼ cup wine. Cook 5 minutes longer. Add remaining ½ cup of wine, salt, black pepper, nutmeg and ginger. Cook until apple is tender and breasts are done. Internal temperature should be at least 165°.

2. Platter breasts, wrap with foil and seal tightly until ready to serve.

3. In small bowl, combine half-and-half, flour, brandy and egg yolks. Mix thoroughly. Add to skillet and simmer until sauce is hot and slightly thickened. Pour over breasts and serve.

NOTES: Date: _____

RATE THIS RECIPE
○ ○ ○ ○ ○

CREAM CHEESE CHICKEN BREASTS

Stove Top

INGREDIENTS

SUBSTITUTIONS

- [ ] 4 – 6 skin-on chicken breasts
- [ ] 3 tablespoons all-purpose flour _____
- [ ] ½ tablespoon ground ginger _____
- [ ] 2 tablespoons extra virgin olive oil _____
- [ ] ¾ cup chicken broth _____
- [ ] 1 package (8 ounce) cream cheese – cubed _____

1. Place flour and ginger in a re-sealable plastic bag. Add breasts and coat thoroughly.

2. Place oil in a large skillet over medium heat. Cook breasts until done. Internal temperature should be at least 165°. Platter breasts, wrap with foil and seal tightly until ready to serve.

3. Reserve drippings in skillet. Add broth to skillet and scrape up browned bits from bottom of skillet. Add cream cheese and simmer over low heat stirring constantly until cheese is melted and sauce thickens.

4. Return breasts to skillet and toss to coat thoroughly with sauce. Simmer 4 – 5 minutes until breasts are heated through.

NOTES: Date: _____

RATE THIS RECIPE
○ ○ ○ ○ ○

CUCUMBERS / MUSHROOMS CHICKEN BREASTS
Stove Top

	INGREDIENTS	SUBSTITUTIONS
☐ 4 – 6	skin-on chicken breasts	
☐ ¼	stick butter	_____
☐ 2	tablespoons extra virgin olive oil	_____
☐ 1	can (4 ounce) sliced mushrooms	_____
☐ 1	garlic clove – minced	_____
☐ ½	teaspoon ground ginger	_____
☐ 4	tablespoons all-purpose flour	_____
☐ 1	cup water	_____
☐ 2	tablespoons brown sauce	_____
☐ 1	large cucumber – cut lengthwise/seeded/sliced	_____
☐ 1	cup sour cream	_____
☐ 1	cucumber – sliced thin (garnish)	_____

1. Melt butter in a large skillet and add oil. Add breasts and cook over medium heat until golden brown. Remove breasts and set aside. Add mushrooms, garlic and ginger to drippings and sauté 2 – 3 minutes.

2. Stir in flour until mushrooms are coated. Blend in water and brown sauce. Bring to a boil over medium heat stirring continuously. Taste, adjust flavoring.

3. Return breasts to skillet. Reduce heat, cover skillet and simmer 15 minutes stirring occasionally.

4. Cut one cucumber into thin slices and set aside as garnish. Peel remaining cucumber. Slice in half lengthwise and remove seeds. Slice crosswise into ½ inch wide slices. Add cucumber to skillet and simmer until breasts are done. Internal temperature should be at least 165°. Remove breasts and wrap with aluminum foil.

5. Stir sour cream into sauce in skillet. Simmer until warm but do not boil. Spoon sauce over breasts and garnish with thinly sliced cucumbers

NOTES: Date: _____

RATE THIS RECIPE
○ ○ ○ ○ ○

CURRY / COCONUT CHICKEN BREASTS

Stove Top | Flattened

		INGREDIENTS	SUBSTITUTIONS
☐	4 – 6	skinless chicken breasts	
☐	¼	teaspoon salt	_____
☐	½	teaspoon black pepper	_____
☐	1	tablespoon extra virgin olive oil	_____
☐	2	green onions – chopped	_____
☐	½	can (8 ounce) crushed pineapple	_____
☐	1	tablespoon curry paste	_____
☐	½	cup chicken broth	_____
☐	½	cup coconut milk	_____
☐	1	tablespoon lime juice	_____
☐	2	teaspoons cilantro – chopped (garnish)	_____

1. Place each breast between sheets of plastic wrap and gently pound flat to an even 1 – 1½ inch thickness. Season with salt and black pepper.

2. Place oil in a large skillet over medium-high heat. Cook breasts until done. Internal temperature should be at least 165°. Set aside.

3. Stir green onions, pineapple and curry paste into skillet and cook 2 minutes stirring frequently. Add broth to skillet and scrape up brown bits. Bring to a full boil and cook until mixture has thickened, 8 –10 minutes. Pour in coconut milk, bring to a boil and cook until thickened. Blend lime juice into sauce. Return breasts to skillet and toss breasts to coat thoroughly. Simmer until warmed through. Garnish with cilantro.

NOTES: Date: _____

RATE THIS RECIPE
○ ○ ○ ○ ○

DILL / CREAM CHICKEN BREASTS
Stove Top

	INGREDIENTS	SUBSTITUTIONS
☐ 4 – 6	skin-on chicken breasts	
☐ ¼	teaspoon salt	_____
☐ ½	teaspoon black pepper	_____
☐ ¼	stick butter	_____
☐ ½	cup chicken broth	_____
☐ ½	cup half-and-half	_____
☐ 1	tablespoon all-purpose flour	_____
☐ 1½	teaspoons dill weed	_____

1. Sprinkle breasts with salt and black pepper. Melt butter in a large skillet over medium heat. Add breasts and cook until golden brown. Reduce heat to low.

2. Add broth. Cover and simmer until breasts are done. Internal temperature should be at least 165°.

3. Platter breasts, wrap with foil and seal tightly until ready to serve.

4. In small bowl, combine half-and-half, flour and dill weed and mix thoroughly. Add flour mixture to skillet. Cook on medium heat stirring until mixture is thickened. Spoon sauce over breasts.

NOTES: Date: _____

RATE THIS RECIPE
○ ○ ○ ○ ○

LIME / BUTTER CHICKEN BREASTS

Stove Top | Flattened

		INGREDIENTS	SUBSTITUTIONS
☐	4 – 6	skinless chicken breasts	
☐	¼	teaspoon salt	_____
☐	½	teaspoon black pepper	_____
☐	1	egg	_____
☐	1	cup dry bread crumbs	_____
☐	2	tablespoons extra virgin olive oil	_____
☐	¼	cup lime juice	_____
☐	6	tablespoons butter	_____
☐	½	teaspoon dried dill weed	_____
☐	1	teaspoon minced chives	_____

1. Place each breast between sheets of plastic wrap and gently pound flat to an even 1 – 1½ inch thickness. Season with salt and black pepper. Place bread crumbs in a re-sealable plastic bag. Whisk egg in a bowl. Dredge breasts with egg. Add breasts to bag and coat in bread crumbs.

2. Place oil in a large skillet over medium heat. Add breasts and cook 4 – 6 minutes on each side until done. Internal temperature should be at least 165°. Wrap with foil and set aside.

3. Add lime juice to skillet. Bring to a boil over low heat. Add butter and stir until melted. Add dill and chives. Spoon sauce over breasts and serve.

NOTES: Date: _____

RATE THIS RECIPE
○ ○ ○ ○ ○

MUSHROOM / RED WINE CHICKEN BREASTS
Stove Top | Flattened

	INGREDIENTS	SUBSTITUTIONS
☐ 4 – 6	skin-on chicken breasts	
☐ ¼	cup all-purpose flour	_____
☐ ¼	cup dry bread crumbs – fine	_____
☐ ½	teaspoon ground ginger	_____
☐ ¼	teaspoon salt	_____
☐ ¼	teaspoon black pepper	_____
☐ ½	teaspoon basil – dried	_____
☐ ½	stick butter	_____
☐ 1	cup fresh mushrooms – sliced	_____
☐ ½	cup red wine	_____

1. Place each breast between sheets of plastic wrap and gently pound flat to an even 1 – 1½ inch thickness.

2. In a re-sealable plastic bag, combine flour, bread crumbs, ginger, salt, black pepper and basil and mix well. Add breasts and coat thoroughly.

3. Heat butter in large skillet over medium heat. Cook breasts until golden brown.

4. Add mushrooms and turn breasts. Cook another 3 – 4 minutes. Add wine to pan. Reduce heat to medium-low. Cover and simmer until breasts are done. Internal temperature should be at least 165°.

5. Platter breasts, wrap with foil and seal tightly until ready to serve.

NOTES: Date: _____

RATE THIS RECIPE
○ ○ ○ ○ ○

MUSHROOM / SPINACH CHICKEN BREASTS
Stove Top | Marinate

		INGREDIENTS	SUBSTITUTIONS
☐	4 – 6	skin-on chicken breasts	
☐	½	cup all-purpose flour	_____
☐	¼	teaspoon salt	_____
☐	3	tablespoons Parmesan cheese – grated	_____
☐	⅓	cup dry bread crumbs – fine	_____
☐	2	eggs – beaten	_____
☐	1	tablespoon milk	_____
☐	6	tablespoons butter – divided	_____
☐	1	bag (16 ounce) frozen spinach	_____
☐	1	tablespoon lemon juice	_____
☐	8	ounces mushrooms – sliced	_____

1. Mix flour and salt in a re-sealable plastic bag. Add breasts and toss to coat thoroughly.

2. Combine cheese with bread crumbs in another re-sealable plastic bag. Pierce each breast 6 – 8 times with a fork. In a bowl, whisk eggs with milk and blend. Dip breasts in egg mixture and add to Parmesan/crumb bag. Turn and toss to coat breasts thoroughly. Press exterior of bag firmly to press mixture onto breasts. Refrigerate 3 hours. Turn bag occasionally to coat breasts evenly.

3. In a large skillet over medium-high heat, melt 4 tablespoons butter. Cook breasts on both sides until browned. Reduce heat and cook breasts covered until done. Internal temperature should be at least 165°. Platter breasts, wrap with foil and seal tightly.

4. Place spinach in a saucepan and bring to a boil. Drain. Add lemon juice to spinach. Place on a serving platter. Arrange cooked breasts over spinach. Cover with aluminum foil to maintain warmth.

5. Heat remaining 2 tablespoons butter in a skillet. Add mushrooms and cook until mushrooms are tender. Spoon mushrooms and butter over breasts and spinach.

NOTES:　　　　　　　　　　　　　　　　Date: _____

RATE THIS RECIPE
○ ○ ○ ○ ○

MUSHROOM / WHITE WINE CHICKEN BREASTS
Stove Top

	INGREDIENTS	SUBSTITUTIONS
☐ 4 – 6	skin-on chicken breasts	
☐ ¾	cup all-purpose flour plus 1 tablespoon	_____
☐ ¼	teaspoon salt	_____
☐ ¼	teaspoon black pepper	_____
☐ ½	teaspoon dried tarragon	_____
☐ 3	eggs – beaten	_____
☐ 1	tablespoon water	_____
☐ 3	tablespoons extra virgin olive oil – divided	_____
☐ 8	ounces mushrooms – sliced	_____
☐ 3	tablespoons butter – divided	_____
☐ ½	can (14 ounce) chicken broth	_____
☐ ½	cup dry white wine	_____
☐ 2	tablespoons lemon juice	_____

1. Combine ¾ cup flour, salt, black pepper and tarragon in a re-sealable plastic bag. In a shallow bowl, whisk together eggs and water. Dip breasts into mixture and coat well. Add breasts to bag and coat well.

2. Place 2 tablespoons oil in large skillet over medium heat. Cook breasts on both sides until done. Internal temperature should be at least 165°. Platter breasts, wrap with foil and seal tightly.

3. Add mushrooms, 1 tablespoon oil and 2 tablespoons butter to skillet. Sauté until mushrooms are browned. Add broth, wine and lemon juice. Simmer on medium heat 3 – 4 minutes to reduce mixture.

4. Combine 1 tablespoon flour with 1 tablespoon butter in a bowl, stirring until smooth. Add to skillet stirring and cooking 1 – 2 minutes until thickened.

5. Return breasts to skillet. Heat and serve.

NOTES: Date: _____

RATE THIS RECIPE
○ ○ ○ ○ ○

ONION SAUCE CHICKEN BREASTS
Stove Top

INGREDIENTS   **SUBSTITUTIONS**

- [ ] 4 – 6 skin-on chicken breasts
- [ ] 1 teaspoon salt – divided
- [ ] ½ teaspoon black pepper
- [ ] ½ cup all-purpose flour plus 1 tablespoon
- [ ] 1 tablespoon extra virgin olive oil
- [ ] 3 shallots – finely chopped
- [ ] ½ cup dry white wine
- [ ] 1 can (14 ounce) chicken broth
- [ ] ½ cup sour cream
- [ ] 1 tablespoon Dijon mustard
- [ ] 5 green onions – white only/finely chopped

1. Sprinkle breasts with ½ teaspoon salt and black pepper. Place ½ cup flour in a re-sealable plastic bag. Add breasts and coat thoroughly.

2. Place oil in skillet over medium-high heat and cook breasts until golden brown and set aside.

3. Add shallots to skillet and cook until golden brown scraping up any browned bits from skillet bottom. Sprinkle 1 tablespoon flour over shallots. Blend thoroughly. Add wine, broth and ½ teaspoon salt. Bring to a boil.

4. Reduce heat and return breasts to skillet and cook until done. Internal temperature should be at least 165°.

5. Platter breasts, wrap with foil and seal tightly until ready to serve.

6. Stir sour cream and mustard into skillet until smooth. Fold onions thoroughly into sauce and spoon over breasts.

NOTES: Date: _____

RATE THIS RECIPE
○ ○ ○ ○ ○

ONION / SOUR CREAM CHICKEN BREASTS
Stove Top

		INGREDIENTS	SUBSTITUTIONS
☐	4 – 6	skin-on chicken breasts	
☐	½	cup all-purpose flour	_____
☐	¼	cup dry bread crumbs - fine	_____
☐	2	teaspoons paprika	_____
☐	½	teaspoon garlic powder	_____
☐	1	teaspoon ground ginger	_____
☐	1	teaspoon black pepper	_____
☐	½	teaspoon ground red pepper	_____
☐	1	stick butter	_____
☐	1	can (10.25 ounce) cream of onion soup	_____
☐	4	scallions – white only/sliced	_____
☐	1	cup sour cream	_____

1. Combine flour, bread crumbs, paprika, garlic powder, ginger, black pepper and red pepper in a re-sealable plastic bag. Add breasts and coat thoroughly.

2. Melt butter in a large skillet over medium-high heat. Cook breasts until browned on both sides. Remove breasts from skillet. Set aside.

3. Add onion soup and scallions to skillet and bring to a near-boil. Return breasts to skillet. Reduce heat to low. Cover and simmer until breasts are done. Baste with pan juices several times. Internal temperature should be at least 165°.

4. Stir in sour cream and blend thoroughly. Warm but do not boil.

NOTES: Date: _____

RATE THIS RECIPE
○ ○ ○ ○ ○

ORANGE / GARLIC CHICKEN BREASTS
Stove Top

		INGREDIENTS	SUBSTITUTIONS
☐	4 – 6	skin-on chicken breasts	
☐	¼	teaspoon salt	_____
☐	½	teaspoon black pepper	_____
☐	1	tablespoon extra virgin olive oil	_____
☐	2	scallions – white only/thinly sliced	_____
☐	8	garlic cloves – minced	_____
☐	¼	cup chicken broth	_____
☐	¼	cup orange juice	_____
☐	¼	teaspoon hot pepper sauce	_____

1. Sprinkle breasts with salt and black pepper. Heat oil in a large skillet over medium-low heat. Add scallions and garlic. Sauté until scallions are limp.

2. Add breasts and cook until golden brown. Remove breasts and set aside.

3. Add broth, orange juice and hot sauce to skillet. Bring to a boil uncovered. Reduce heat and simmer 5 minutes to reduce mixture.

4. Return breasts to skillet, cover and simmer over low heat until breasts are done. Internal temperature should be at least 165°.

5. Platter breasts, wrap with foil and seal tightly until ready to serve.

NOTES: Date: _____

RATE THIS RECIPE
○ ○ ○ ○ ○

PISTACHIO / SCOTCH WHISKEY CHICKEN BREASTS
Stove Top

	INGREDIENTS	SUBSTITUTIONS
☐ 4 – 6	skin-on chicken breasts	
☐ ¾	cup pistachio nuts – finely crushed	_____
☐ ½	cup dry bread crumbs – fine	_____
☐ ¼	teaspoon black pepper	_____
☐ 2	tablespoons extra virgin olive oil	_____
☐ 1	stick butter – divided	_____
☐ 3	tablespoons Dijon mustard	_____
☐ ½	cup brown sugar – packed	_____
☐ ½	cup Scotch whiskey	_____
☐ 2	teaspoons Worcestershire sauce	_____
☐ 2	teaspoons soy sauce	_____

1. Blend nuts, bread crumbs and black pepper in a re-sealable plastic bag.

2. Brush breasts liberally with oil. Add breasts to bag and toss to coat thoroughly. Press sides of bag firmly to adhere mixture to breasts.

3. Place 2 tablespoons butter in large skillet on medium high heat. Cook breasts until done. Internal temperature should be at least 165°. Cover skillet. Reduce heat to low and keep breasts warm.

4. In a saucepan, combine mustard, brown sugar, Scotch, Worcestershire and soy sauce. Blend thoroughly and bring to a simmer. Melt remaining butter into mixture. Mix thoroughly.

5. Pour sauce over breasts and serve.

NOTES: Date: _____

RATE THIS RECIPE
○ ○ ○ ○ ○

SESAME SEED CHICKEN BREASTS
Stove Top | Flattened

		INGREDIENTS	SUBSTITUTIONS
☐	4 – 6	skin-on chicken breasts	
☐	2	teaspoons extra virgin olive oil	_____
☐	3	teaspoons sesame seeds	_____
☐	¼	teaspoon salt	_____
☐	½	teaspoon black pepper	_____
☐	2	teaspoons Dijon mustard	_____
☐	⅔	cup chicken broth	_____
☐	1	teaspoon cornstarch	_____

1. Place each breast between sheets of plastic wrap and gently pound flat to an even 1 – 1½ inch thickness.

2. In a large skillet, heat oil over medium heat. Toast sesame seeds, stirring 1 minute. Remove seeds and set aside.

3. Season breasts with salt and black pepper. Add breasts to skillet. Cook until done. Internal temperature should be at least 165°. Coat with toasted sesame seeds. Platter breasts, wrap with foil and seal tightly until ready to serve.

4. In a bowl, whisk together Dijon mustard, broth and cornstarch. Slowly add broth mixture to skillet. Cook and stir until thickened. Pour over breasts and serve.

NOTES: Date: _____

RATE THIS RECIPE
○ ○ ○ ○ ○

TARRAGON / CREAM CHICKEN BREASTS
Stove Top

	INGREDIENTS	SUBSTITUTIONS
☐ 4 – 6	skin-on chicken breasts	
☐ 4	tablespoons all-purpose flour – divided	_____
☐ ½	tablespoon ground ginger	_____
☐ ¼	teaspoon salt	_____
☐ ¼	teaspoon black pepper	_____
☐ 5	tablespoons butter – divided	_____
☐ 1	small onion – finely chopped	_____
☐ ¼	cup dry white wine	_____
☐ ¾	teaspoon dried tarragon	_____
☐ ¼	cup chicken broth	_____
☐ ¼	cup half-and-half	_____

1. Place 3 tablespoons flour, ginger, salt and black pepper in a resealable plastic bag. Add breasts and toss to coat completely.

2. In a large skillet, heat 3 tablespoons butter over medium heat. Add breasts and cook on both sides until golden brown. Remove breasts from skillet and wrap tightly in aluminum foil.

3. Add onion to skillet and sauté until wilted and translucent. Add wine to skillet. Increase heat to high and cook until liquid is reduced by half. Reduce heat to medium-low. Add 1 tablespoon flour to skillet and blend until thickened. Add tarragon and broth.

4. Return breasts to skillet. Cover and simmer on low heat until done. Internal temperature should be at least 165°. Platter breasts and wrap with aluminum foil.

5. Add 2 tablespoons butter and half-and-half to skillet. Heat through but do not boil. Spoon sauce over breasts and serve.

NOTES: Date: _____

RATE THIS RECIPE
○ ○ ○ ○ ○

VEGETABLE CHICKEN BREASTS
Stove Top

		INGREDIENTS	SUBSTITUTIONS
☐	4 – 6	skin-on chicken breasts	
☐	2	tablespoons extra virgin olive oil	_____
☐	1	medium onion – chopped	_____
☐	3	garlic cloves – minced	_____
☐	½	green bell pepper – chopped	_____
☐	1	can (28 ounce) diced tomatoes	_____
☐	1	can (8 ounce) tomato sauce	_____
☐	½	cup red wine	_____
☐	¼	teaspoon salt	_____
☐	½	teaspoon black pepper	_____
☐	½	teaspoon allspice	_____
☐	2	bay leaves	_____
☐	¼	teaspoon cayenne pepper	_____

1. Pour oil in a large skillet over medium heat. Add breasts and cook until golden brown. Set breasts aside.

2. Add onion, garlic and bell pepper to skillet and sauté until onion is wilted and translucent.

3. Add other ingredients and breasts to skillet. Simmer on low until breasts are done. Remove bay leaves. Internal temperature should be at least 165°.

NOTES: Date: _____

RATE THIS RECIPE
○ ○ ○ ○ ○

NOTES

SLOW COOKER CHICKEN BREASTS

CREAM CHEESE / ITALIAN CHICKEN BREASTS
Slow Cooker

	INGREDIENTS	SUBSTITUTIONS
☐ 4 – 6	skin-on chicken breasts	
☐ 1	envelope (.7 ounce) Italian salad dressing mix	_____
☐ ⅓	cup water	_____
☐ 1	package (8 ounce) cream cheese	_____
☐ 1	can (10.75 ounce) cream of chicken soup	_____
☐ 1	can (4 ounce) mushrooms – stems/pieces – drained	_____
☐ 2	cups cooked rice	_____

1. Combine salad dressing mix and water in slow cooker and blend thoroughly. Add breasts and coat thoroughly.

2. Whisk together cream cheese and soup in a small bowl until blended. Stir in mushrooms. Pour cream cheese mixture over breasts. Toss breasts to coat thoroughly.

3. Cook on low 6 – 8 hours until done. Internal temperature should be at least 165°. Slow cooking requires internal heat and condensation. Resist removing lid too often.

4. Serve over cooked rice.

NOTES: Date: _____

RATE THIS RECIPE
○ ○ ○ ○ ○

CREOLE SAUCE CHICKEN BREASTS
Slow Cooker

	INGREDIENTS	SUBSTITUTIONS
☐ 4 – 6	skin-on chicken breasts	
☐ 3	tablespoons butter	_____
☐ 8	scallions – white only/sliced thin	_____
☐ 2	bacon slices	_____
☐ 4	tablespoons all-purpose flour	_____
☐ 1	teaspoon Cajun seasoning	_____
☐ ¾	cup chicken broth	_____
☐ 2	tablespoons tomato paste	_____
☐ ½	cup half-and-half	_____
☐	cooked noodles for 4	_____

1. Cut bacon into 1 inch squares. Melt butter in a saucepan over medium heat. Add bacon and scallions. Cook until bacon is crisp and scallions are limp.

2. Add flour and Cajun seasoning to saucepan. Stir and cook 2 minutes. Add chicken broth and cook over medium heat until mixture is slightly thickened. Add tomato paste and blend thoroughly.

3. Place breasts in slow cooker. Add sauce mixture. Cover and cook on low 6 – 8 hours until done. Internal temperature should be at least 165°. Resist removing lid too often. Slow cooking requires internal heat and condensation. Stir once during cooking.

4. Stir in half-and-half about 30 minutes before done. Serve over cooked noodles.

NOTES: Date: _____

RATE THIS RECIPE
○ ○ ○ ○ ○

DRIED CHIPPED BEEF CHICKEN BREASTS
Slow Cooker

		INGREDIENTS	SUBSTITUTIONS
☐	4 – 6	skin-on chicken breasts	
☐	¼	teaspoon black pepper	_____
☐	¼	teaspoon garlic powder	_____
☐	¼	teaspoon ground ginger	_____
☐	1	can (10.5 ounce) cream of mushroom soup	_____
☐	½	cup sour cream	_____
☐	¼	cup chicken broth	_____
☐	1	jar (6 ounce) dried chipped beef – diced	_____

1. Place black pepper, garlic powder, ginger, soup, sour cream, broth and dried beef in slow cooker. Mix thoroughly. Add breasts and coat thoroughly.

2. Cover and cook on low 6 – 8 hours until done. Internal temperature should be at least 165°. Resist removing lid too often. Slow cooking requires internal heat and condensation.

3. Platter breasts, wrap with foil and seal tightly until ready to serve.

NOTES: Date: _____

RATE THIS RECIPE
○ ○ ○ ○ ○

NOTES

APPENDIX

PLAYING WITH FIRE (INSIDE)

There are numerous methods for applying heat to food, thus turning it from tartar to terrific. Below are tips and tricks for effectively and safely performing this common-place yet profound metamorphosis indoors.

OVEN COOKING

Consider these tips:

- Oven mitts are mandatory and should always be kept where they are easily accessible. You run the risk of serious injury if you forget to glove your hand before thrusting said hand into the inferno of the oven and grabbing a hot handle.

- Preheating the oven is essential when following recommended cooking temperatures in recipes. If the oven is not at the recommended temp when you begin cooking the dish, the results may be less than palatable.

- Place the oven racks in the proper position before you preheat the oven. If you wait to move the rack after heating, you will be moving a hot oven rack and could potentially burn yourself.

- Double check the temperature settings before placing the dish in the oven.

- Utensils need to be ovenproof. If the tool is not ovenproof, it may melt when placed in a hot oven.

- When oven cooking with a sheet pan or broiling pan, line it with aluminum foil first. Spray the foil with no-stick cooking oil. Using foil will protect the pan from baked-on ingredients. Recipes with sugar products—white sugar, brown sugar, maple syrup, corn syrup or molasses—will burn hard onto the pan surface if it is not protected, sometimes to the point where it is easier to throw the pan out than clean it.

- Some recipes call for cooking the dish both covered and uncovered at different times in the cooking process. For best results, follow the instructions carefully.

Oven temperatures are often classified into categories. Here are the distinctions that I like to use:

250° – 300°	Low
301° – 350°	Medium
351° – 425°	Hot
426° – 475°	Very Hot
476° plus	Whatcha got yourself there, a nuclear reactor?

STOVE TOP COOKING

- The best stove top cooking happens when the correct size burner is used. Use small pots, pans and skillets on the small burners, and larger vessels on the larger burners.

- Make sure the temperature setting is correct. A high setting when the recipe calls for a low setting will ruin a dish quickly.

- Keep cooking utensils and ingredients in a location that won't require reaching across the burners or cooking vessels.

- When braising or sautéing food in a saucepan, the splattering of the butter or oil can cause serious burns. To minimize that chance, slightly lift the edge of the skillet that is closest to you and work with the ingredients at the back of the skillet.

- Consider when a lid cover or a splatter screen might be useful. Both minimize grease splatters, protecting you from burns. Bonus: will help keep the stove top and counters clean.

SLOW COOKER / CROCK-POT COOKING

The terms "slow cooker" and "crock-pot" are synonymous and refer to the same hardware. The lowest setting is generally about 200° and the high setting is about 300°. One cooking hour on high is roughly equivalent to two cooking hours on low. Many recipes that call for the "low" setting will go for approximately 8 hours, and if the recipes calls for "high," it is a good bet the recommended cooking time will be 3 – 4 hours.

To obtain the best dishes, the slow cooker must be no more than two-thirds full. Half full is fine. Steam creates a vacuum that seals the lid and the lid needs a tight fit to form a vacuum. If filled to the brim, the top will most likely not seal correctly.

Opening the lid prolongs the cooking time. Each time you remove the lid, it can add up to 15 minutes to the cooking time.

Some recipes suggest stirring the dish halfway through cooking. Stir quickly and replace the lid quickly.

Here are some tips for producing successful slow cooker dishes:

- Selecting cheaper cuts of meat is actually preferable when using a slow cooker. They have less fat, and the long, moist cooking turns what are normally tough cuts into tender treats.
- Remove poultry skin and excess fat. The fat melts with the slow cooking process and adds a distinctly unpleasant flavor and texture to the dish.
- Cut meat and poultry into cube pieces. This will ensure thorough cooking.
- Defrost foods before cooking.
- Foods at the bottom of the crock-pot cook at slightly higher temperatures. Pay attention to this when loading the vessel. For instance, when cooking a dish with meat and root vegetables, placing the vegetables on the bottom and the meat on top will help all the ingredients come to doneness at the same time.

- To ramp up the flavors, the liquid can be concentrated by cranking the slow cooker up to high for the last half hour.
- To prevent dairy products (sour cream, heavy cream, yogurt, milk) from breaking down, add during the last 15 minutes of cooking.
- The ceramic insert of the slow cooker can be damaged by sudden temperature changes. It should not be immersed in water while still hot from cooking, or taken from the refrigerator and placed into a preheated base.
- Exercise care when cleaning the ceramic insert. Let the insert cool before immersing it in water. Use a soft cloth and warm, soapy water to clean the insert. Do not use any harsh cleaners or abrasive cleansing pads. Do not immerse the slow cooker heating element or the cord in water, and keep the unit unplugged when not in use.

PLAYING WITH FIRE (OUTSIDE)

There is something primal about grilling food outdoors. The open air, the billowing fragrant smoke, the constant tending of the grill temperature, and the elaborate, almost ritual poking and prodding of the food. Below are tips and tricks for maximizing the grilling experience that have worked for me over the years.

ABOUT COALS

Open the vents on the bottom of the grill. Light a large chimney starter full of charcoal. If you don't own a chimney starter, I highly recommend you acquire one.

When the coals are glowing grayish white (start checking coals after 15 minutes), the coals are at their hottest. Spread the coals on the lower grate.

Positioning coals is critical for controlling the grill heat. Use long handled tongs to spread the coals around the lower grate. Leave a little space between coals.

THREE GRILLING METHODS

Here are three different tried-and-true grilling methods that are effective for just about any grilling situation. The methods are direct heat, indirect heat and tri-divided heat.

DIRECT HEAT

For even temperature distribution, spread the coals uniformly over the coal grate, at a depth of one or two coals. Open the bottom vents. Open the top vents if grilling with the cover on.

INDIRECT HEAT

This is the best method for barbecuing or slow roasting. The cooking is done with the grill covered and the meat grilled for an extended period, sometimes with wood chips to impart a smoked flavor.

Place an aluminum drip pan in the center of the charcoal grate. Light the coals and, when the coals are covered with gray ash, place the coals around the drip pan. Water can be added to the pan to provide moisture. Do not place meat directly over coals when grilling with indirect heat.

The temperature of the grill can be controlled by manipulating the upper and lower vents. The temperature for low-indirect cooking should be kept at approximately 275° for the entire cooking period. Use a grill thermometer to determine actual temperatures.

If you are using wood chips, leave the cover slightly ajar to draw smoke upward over the meat.

TRI-DIVIDED HEAT

The third grilling method is to divide the coal grate into three sections. Place the coals that will provide the heat area for searing in section one, to the far left. The second section is a coal-free cooking area in the center, next to the burning coals. When grilling in the second section, the meat will not be directly above the coals. The third section of the grill is also coal-free and has less heat and is some distance from the coals. This is a good area for resting meats, and is an area to move the meat in the event of flare-ups.

GRILL HEAT CONTROL

Avoid lifting the grill cover too often. When the cover is lifted, the temperature drops significantly and the cooking time is extended. Use a grill thermometer to determine actual grill temperature.

HEAT TOO HIGH

If grill heat is too high, there are actions that can be taken to reduce the heat. The first is to use long handled tongs to scatter coals. Move the food to the coolest section of the grill. The vents, top and bottom, should be closed or nearly closed to starve the charcoal of oxygen.

HEAT TOO LOW

If the heat is too low, there are several things you can do to increase the heat. The first is to consolidate the coals by stacking them all in one place and adding more charcoal, preheated if possible. If the coals are not pre-heated, place the fresh coals on the hot collection of coals. Fan the coals with a newspaper. Lastly, open all the vents to provide plenty of oxygen.

If you are in a northern climate during the winter, clear the grill of any snow and provide more time for preheating. Increase the recommended cooking temperature by 15% – 20% to allow for the chill. Do not grill in an enclosed environment such as a basement or garage as deadly carbon monoxide gases can be trapped.

GAS GRILLS

Preheat all burners on high, cover the grill with the lid and heat for 10 minutes and then adjust heat according to recipe. For indirect heat cooking, turn off one burner. Turn off the middle burner if there are three. Always have a backup tank of gas.

GRILL SAFETY

- Place the grill well away from existing structures, deck railings, house eaves and trees.
- Place the grill a safe distance from other activities, especially foot traffic.
- Grills are designed to be used out-of-doors only. Indoor use poses both a fire hazard and the risk of carbon monoxide exposure.
- Always use long-handled grilling tools to give you plenty of clearance from heat and flames when cooking.
- Excess grease buildup in your grill is a fire hazard and will contribute to flare-ups while cooking, if not outright fire. Be sure to clean your grill periodically.

AVOIDING THE EMERGENCY ROOM

RUDE POISONING

Food poisoning (Food Borne Illness) is nasty and potentially deadly. Most preventable cases of food poisoning are caused by cross-contamination from raw meat, poultry, seafood and dairy products (a.k.a. "proteins").

Food safety issues occur when food is between the temperatures of 40° and 140° – the Food Danger Zone. Cooked food should never be allowed to remain in the danger zone for more than a couple of hours at most. Foods in the danger zone are a breeding ground for the bacteria and other toxins responsible for food-borne illnesses.

If food poisoning occurs in your home, take note of the foods eaten and then freeze any uneaten portions. The frozen samples may need to be tested in order to identify the offending bug and appropriate medical treatment.

When safety of the protein is in doubt, *discard it*. Always err on the side of safety.

SAFE HANDLING OF PROTEINS

- Refrigerate proteins promptly after purchase.
- Raw proteins should never be left out at room temperature.
- Packaged proteins can be refrigerated in the original packaging.
- Freeze uncooked proteins if they will not be used within 2 days.
- Proteins will take from 4 – 10 hours to thaw in the refrigerator. Do not thaw proteins on the counter top.
- To thaw proteins in cold water, place in a watertight plastic bag and change water frequently.
- The microwave can be used to thaw most proteins. Thawing seafood in the microwave is not recommended.
- Frozen, uncooked proteins such as meat and poultry should be used within two or three months of freezing. Frozen cooked protein should be used within a month of freezing. Freezing seafood – cooked or uncooked – is not recommended unless it is professionally frozen.

AVOIDING CROSS-CONTAMINATION

- Uncooked protein should be kept separate from produce, cooked foods and ready-to-eat foods.
- Never place cooked food on a plate that previously held uncooked protein.

- If you intend to use the marinade as a sauce, (1) keep a portion of the unused marinade separate for use on the cooked protein, or (2) place the used marinade in a sauce pan and bring it to a boil. Reduce heat and simmer for 4 – 5 minutes.
- Use one cutting board for fresh produce, such as vegetables and fruits, and a different one for raw proteins. If you must use only one cutting board, wash it thoroughly with hot, soapy water after using with raw proteins.
- Using hot soapy water, wash your hands, dishes, knives and other utensils thoroughly after coming in contact with uncooked proteins. For cutting boards and counters, use a hot soapy water scrub followed by a rinse solution of one tablespoon liquid bleach to one gallon water. Rinse with water.

COOKING TEMPERATURES

Cooking times listed in recipes are approximations. A meat thermometer is a necessary piece of cooking equipment for ensuring the proper internal temperature of foods. Always use this critical piece of cooking hardware to monitor internal temperatures.

See Table 5 in the Appendix[1] for recommended safe internal temperatures for cooked meats.

STOP, DROP AND ROLL

Cooking is the leading cause of home fires and home fire injuries in the United States. Taking proper precautions and learning what to do in case of a kitchen fire can prevent property damage, injury, and potentially save lives.

- Do not leave pots and pans unattended on the stove or in the oven. Most home fires are the result of unattended cooking. Turn pan handles on the stove towards the back to prevent food spills or children accidentally grabbing the handles.

- Pot holders and towels should be kept away from stove tops and ovens. Bathrobes, aprons and loose clothing are highly susceptible to catching fire. If clothing catches fire, immediately stop, drop to the ground and roll to smother the fire.
- In case of fire, turn off the burner under the burning pot or pan. Cover the fire with a large lid. Leave the lid on until the pan cools. Turn off the hood fan so fire is not drawn into the ducts.
- Always, *always* have a properly rated fire extinguisher within arms reach. Familiarize yourself with the instructions and practice a dry-run so you can operate it if and when needed.
- Never, *never* attempt to put out a grease fire with water. You will only cause the oil to erupt and this will spread the fire around the kitchen, and, in all probability, throughout the house. Use a Class B extinguisher.[2] (Most household fire extinguishers are Class ABC, so are appropriate.)
- Call 911 in the event of a fire.

NOTES

TABLES

TABLE 1: HERB AND SPICE SUBSTITUTIONS

RECIPE CALLS FOR	OPTION 1	OPTION 2
Allspice	cinnamon with a dash of nutmeg	dash of cloves
Basil	oregano	thyme
Cajun Spice	combine white pepper, garlic powder, onion powder, ground red pepper, paprika and black pepper	
Chili Powder	dashes of hot pepper sauce, oregano and cumin	
Chive	green onion	leek
Cilantro	parsley	
Italian Seasoning	blend of basil, oregano, rosemary and ground red pepper	
Cinnamon	nutmeg	allspice
Cloves	cinnamon	nutmeg
Cumin	chili powder	
Garlic, 1 clove	¼ teaspoon garlic powder	½ teaspoon prepared minced garlic
Ginger	allspice	cinnamon
Horseradish, 1 tablespoon fresh	2 tablespoons bottled	
Hot pepper sauce, 1 teaspoon	¾ teaspoon cayenne pepper plus 1 teaspoon vinegar	
Marjoram	basil	thyme
Mustard prepared, 1 tablespoon	1 teaspoon dry mustard	
Mustard dry, 1 teaspoon	1 tablespoon prepared mustard	

RECIPE CALLS FOR	OPTION 1	OPTION 2
Mustard Dijon, 1 tablespoon	1 tablespoon dry mustard mixed with 1 teaspoon white wine vinegar, 1 tablespoon mayonnaise, and a pinch of sugar	
Nutmeg	cinnamon	ginger
Oregano	thyme	basil
Parsley, ¼ cup chopped fresh	1 tablespoon dried parsley flakes	¼ cup chopped cilantro
Poultry Seasoning	sage plus a blend of thyme, marjoram, black pepper, and rosemary	
Red Pepper	dash of hot pepper sauce	black pepper
Rosemary	thyme	tarragon
Sage	poultry seasoning	marjoram
Thyme	basil	oregano

TABLE 2: COMMON INGREDIENT SUBSTITUTIONS

RECIPE CALLS FOR	ALTERNATIVE
Broth, beef or chicken, 1 cup	1 bouillon cube dissolved in 1 cup boiling water
Coconut milk, 1 cup	3 tablespoons canned cream of coconut plus enough milk to equal 1 cup
Cornstarch, 1 tablespoon	2 tablespoon all-purpose flour
Corn syrup	honey
Cream, half-and-half, 1 cup	½ cup whole milk, plus ½ cup light cream
Cream cheese	cottage cheese, puréed
Green onions	onion
Honey, 1 cup	1¼ cups sugar plus ¼ cup liquid
Leeks	shallots
Lemon juice	vinegar
Maple syrup, 2 cups	honey, 1 cup
Mayonnaise, 1 cup	½ cup yogurt and ½ cup mayonnaise
Mushrooms, 1 pound fresh	6 ounces canned mushrooms
Oil (sauteing), ¼ cup	¼ cup melted butter
Onion, 1 medium	1 tablespoon dried minced onion
Red Pepper	dash of hot pepper sauce
Sour cream, 1 cup	1 cup sour milk and ¼ cup butter
Sugar brown, 1 cup firmly packed	1 cup granulated sugar plus ¼ cup unsulphured molasses
Tomatoes, 1 cup canned	1½ cups chopped tomato, simmered for 10 minutes
Tomato juice, 1 cup	½ cup tomato sauce plus ½ cup water
Tomato ketchup	1 cup tomato sauce plus ½ cup sugar and 2 tablespoons vinegar
Tomato sauce, 2 cups	¾ cup tomato paste plus 1 cup water
Vinegar, Balsamic	sherry vinegar
Vinegar (white or cider)	lemon juice
Worcestershire sauce	bottled steak sauce

TABLE 3: HEALTHY INGREDIENT SUBSTITUTIONS

RECIPE CALLS FOR	HEALTHY ALTERNATIVE
Bacon	turkey bacon, ham, Canadian bacon
Butter	60/40 butter blend with reduced calorie margarine
Cream	skim milk, evaporated skim milk
Cream cheese	yogurt cheese
Egg, 1 whole	2 egg whites
Egg, 2 whole	1 whole egg plus 2 egg whites
Ground beef	ground poultry
Heavy cream, 1 cup	1 tablespoon flour whisked into 1 cup nonfat milk
Mayonnaise	half light mayonnaise and half non-fat yogurt
Meat	legumes, lentils, dried beans or dried peas
Milk, whole	2% milk, 1% milk, skim milk, evaporated milk or soy milk fortified with calcium
Sour cream, 1 cup	1 cup low fat cottage cheese plus 2 tablespoons skim milk plus 1 tablespoon lemon juice
Tuna, canned, oil-packed	canned tuna, water-packed
White bread	100% whole grain or 100% whole wheat bread

TABLE 4: LIQUOR SUBSTITUTIONS

RECIPE CALLS FOR	OPTION 1	OPTION 2
Amaretto	almond extract	marzipan
Apple brandy	apple juice	apple cider
Apricot brandy	apricot preserves	
Beer or Ale	chicken broth	ginger ale
Bourbon	sparkling grape juice	vanilla extract
Brandy	raspberry extract	brandy extract
Champagne	ginger ale	soda water
Cognac	peach juice	apricot juice
Coffee liqueur	espresso	coffee syrup
Creme de Menthe	grapefruit juice	mint extract
Grand Marnier	orange marmalade	orange juice
Peppermint Schnapps	mint extract	mint leaves
Port	cranberry juice plus lemon juice	
Rum	pineapple juice	vanilla extract
Sherry	apple cider	coffee syrup
Vermouth	apple cider	
Vodka	white grape juice plus lime juice	apple cider
Wine, Red	grape juice	cranberry juice
Wine, White	white grape juice	apple juice

TABLE 5: SAFE INTERNAL TEMPERATURES

CUT	MINIMUM SAFE INTERNAL TEMPERATURE
Roasts – Beef, veal, lamb	145° F (medium rare) 160° F (medium)
Fish, shellfish	145° F
Pork	160° F
Ground – beef, lamb, veal	160° F
Egg dishes	160° F
Poultry, any cut	165° F
Leftovers, any meat	165° F

TABLE 6: TRINITY FLAVOR BASES

TRINITY	1	2	3
French (Mirepoix)	celery	onion	carrots
Cajun or Creole (Holy Trinity - 1:2:3 ratio)	onion	bell pepper	celery
Italian	tomato	garlic	basil
Mexican	ancho chili pepper	pasilla chili pepper	guajillo chili pepper
Chinese	scallions	ginger	garlic
Greek	lemon juice	olive oil	oregano
Indian	garlic	ginger	onion
Spanish	garlic	onion	tomato
Thai	galangal	kaffir lime	lemon grass

TABLE 7: PEPPERHEAD SCALE

PEPPER	SCOVILLE HEAT UNITS
Cherry	500
Sonora	600
Coronado	1,000
Polano	2,000
Ancho	2,000
Anaheim	2,500
Chipotle	5,000
Jalapeño	10,000
Serrano	22,000
Tabasco	50,000
Cayenne	50,000
Jamaican Hot	200,000
Chocolate Habanero	425,000
Police Pepper Spray	5,300,000
Pure Capsaicin	16,000,000

TABLE 8: RECOMMENDED CHICKEN GEAR

GEAR	DESCRIPTION
Aluminum foil	12-inch wide works well for lining the baking pan and for covering food after cooking.
Baking pan	A rectangular baking pan is used for baking chicken and sauces together. A heavy duty pan that will not warp works best.
Basting brush	A heavy 2-inch silicone brush with a comfortable 8-inch handle works well.
Extra bag of charcoal	Never run out, never say die
Extra LP tank	Never run out, never say die
Fire Extinguisher	One in the kitchen, one by the grill
Grill thermometer	Helpful for regulating grill temperature.
Heavy knife or heavy scissors	Used for cutting the chicken segments. The heavier and sharper the knife the better. A rigid knife works well. .
Measuring cup	A measuring cup registering standard increments.
Measuring spoons	A complete set of measuring spoons from 1/8 teaspoon to a full tablespoon.
Meat thermometer	Essential for determining when meats are ready to safely eat.
Mixing bowls	Various sizes used for mixing sauces and marinades.
Oven mitts	Used for protection when extracting items from the oven and when working the grill.
Re-sealable plastic bags	Used for coating and marinating meats.
Saucepans	Used for preparing sauce. Saucepans with heavy bottoms work best.
Short- and long-handled Tongs	Used for extracting from marinade and for turning chicken when baking and grilling.

GEAR	DESCRIPTION
Skillets	Used for braising and sauce reduction – a large skillet for braising and a smaller one for sauces. I recommend a stainless steel skillet with an aluminum core.
Spatula	For stirring and coating chicken. Spatulas with tips rigid and large enough to mix and coat a lot of chicken at a time work best.

REFERENCES

[1] Excerpt from USDA Keep Food Safe! Food Safety Basics
http://www.fsis.usda.gov/factsheets/Keep_Food_Safe_Food_Safety_Basics/index.asp

[2] U.S. Fire Administration, Fire Extinguishers
http://www.usfa.dhs.gov/citizens/home_fire_prev/extinguishers.shtm

NOTES

INDEX

A

all-purpose flour 58, 67, 73, 90, 91, 92, 93, 94, 97, 99, 100, 102, 104, 106, 110, 118
allspice 112
apple juice 91
apples 92
artichoke hearts 58

B

bacon 61, 76, 118
basil 34, 39, 41, 76, 99
bay leaves 112
blue cheese 60, 61
brandy 92
bread crumbs 46, 60, 70, 108
bread crumbs, dry 67, 98, 99, 100, 106
brown sauce 94
brown sugar 42, 43, 47, 50, 108
butter 29, 58, 60, 61, 62, 63, 66, 67, 69, 70, 71, 73, 76, 84, 86, 88, 92, 94, 97, 98, 99, 100, 102, 106, 108, 110, 118

C

Cajun seasoning 30, 86, 118
cayenne pepper 34, 84, 112
celery salt 46
celery stalks 83, 89
cheddar cheese 84
cherry tomatoes 86
chicken broth 36, 38, 58, 64, 69, 73, 86, 91, 93, 96, 97, 102, 104, 107, 109, 110, 118, 119
chili powder 32, 89
chipped beef, dried 119
chives 98
cider vinegar 35, 36, 41, 44, 49, 50, 51, 52, 71
cilantro 86, 96
coconut milk 88, 96
Cointreau 90
corn 89

cornstarch 36, 44, 47, 67, 109
cranberries 90, 91
cream cheese 93, 117
cream of chicken soup 117
cream of mushroom soup 67, 68, 119
cream of onion soup 106
cucumber 32, 94
cumin 32, 33
curry paste 96
curry powder 51, 63

D

Dijon mustard 39, 41, 50, 63, 71, 91, 104, 108, 109
dill weed 29, 68, 97, 98
dry mustard 35, 48, 51
dry white wine 65, 83, 86, 92, 102, 104, 110

E

eggs 70, 76, 98, 100, 102
egg yolks 92
extra virgin olive oil 30, 32, 33, 34, 35, 38, 39, 44, 50, 52, 58, 60, 65, 68, 69, 83, 84, 86, 89, 90, 91, 93, 94, 96, 98, 102, 104, 107, 108, 109, 112

G

garlic cloves 30, 34, 35, 42, 48, 49, 50, 52, 62, 65, 66, 83, 84, 89, 94, 107, 112
garlic powder 38, 40, 46, 76, 88, 106, 119
garlic salt 33, 51
ginger 30, 31, 36, 38, 40, 42, 43, 46, 48, 49, 58, 63, 65, 68, 83, 84, 88, 90, 91, 92, 93, 94, 99, 106, 110, 119
ginger, candied 72
green bell peppers 84, 112
green olives 62
green onions 96, 104
ground red pepper 106

H
half-and-half 86, 92, 97, 110, 118
honey 34, 35, 36, 38, 48, 63, 64
hot pepper sauce 42, 52, 107

I
Italian salad dressing 70
Italian salad dressing mix 117

J
jalapeño peppers 89

K
ketchup 47, 51, 52

L
lemonade, frozen 40
lemon juice 29, 31, 36, 39, 46, 47, 50, 58, 62, 65, 68, 100, 102
lemons 65, 66
lemon zest 31, 47, 65
lime juice 50, 89, 96, 98
lime zest 89
liquid smoke 52

M
maple syrup 41, 49
milk 67, 100
mushrooms 58, 67, 68, 73, 94, 99, 100, 102, 117

N
noodles 118
nutmeg 76, 92

O
olives 58
onion 32, 65, 76, 84, 88, 89, 110, 112
onion, dried minced 29
onion powder 30, 38, 48, 67, 83
onion soup mix 68
orange juice 31, 35, 36, 41, 42, 69, 90, 107
orange peel 41
orange zest 31, 36
oregano 34, 35, 45, 52, 65, 70, 76

P
paprika 40, 51, 52, 67, 68, 73, 106
Parmesan cheese 70, 100
parsley 32, 34
peach preserves 71
pineapple 47, 64, 72, 96
pineapple juice 43, 63, 72
pistachio nuts 108

R
raspberry jam 45
raspberry juice, concentrated 44
red bell pepper 86
red pepper flakes 32
red raspberries 45
red wine 45, 99, 112
red wine vinegar 45
rice 117
ricotta cheese 76
rosemary 65, 72
rum extract 42

S
sage 46, 68
salsa 74
scallions 61, 72, 86, 90, 92, 106, 107, 118
Scotch whiskey 108
sesame seeds 109
shallots 104
sour cream 46, 68, 73, 74, 91, 94, 104, 106, 119
soy sauce 36, 38, 40, 42, 43, 44, 108
spinach 76, 88, 100

T
taco season mix 74
tarragon 44, 62, 64, 69, 102, 110
teriyaki marinade 31
thyme 34, 65, 71
tomatoes 58, 89, 112
tomato paste 84, 118
tomato sauce 35, 112
tomato soup 48

W
white rice 84, 89, 90
white sugar 34, 51
white wine 58, 64, 84
Worcestershire sauce 43, 46, 49, 51, 52, 64, 108

Y
yellow bell pepper 32

NOTES

NOTES

NOTES

NOTES

NOTES